P9-BHU-993

Fire in the Bones

Fire in the Bones

WILLIAM TYNDALE —
MARTYR,
FATHER OF THE ENGLISH BIBLE

S. MICHAEL WILCOX

DESERET
BOOK

SALT LAKE CITY, UTAH

© 2004 S. Michael Wilcox

All rights reserved. No part of this book may be reproduced in any form or by any means without permission in writing from the publisher, Deseret Book Company, P. O. Box 30178, Salt Lake City, Utah 84130. This work is not an official publication of The Church of Jesus Christ of Latter-day Saints. The views expressed herein are the responsibility of the author and do not necessarily represent the position of the Church or of Deseret Book Company.

DESERET BOOK is a registered trademark of Deseret Book Company.

Visit us at deseretbook.com

Library of Congress Cataloging-in-Publication Data

Wilcox, S. Michael.
  Fire in the bones : William Tyndale, martyr, father of the English Bible /
S. Michael Wilcox.
    p. cm.
  Includes bibliographical references and index.
  ISBN-10 1-59038-297-8 (hardbound : alk. paper)
  ISBN-13 978-1-59038-297-4 (hardbound : alk. paper)
  1. Tyndale, William, d. 1536. 2. Reformation—England—Biography.
3. Bible. English—Versions—Tyndale. I. Title.
  BR350.T8W47 2004
  270.6'092—dc22
2004006273

Printed in the United States of America
Edwards Brothers, Inc., Ann Arbor, MI

16 15 14 13 12

To Mavis and Farelyn,
dear English friends

But his word was in mine heart

As a burning fire shut up in my bones,

And I was weary with forbearing,

And I could not stay.

—Jeremiah 20:9

And if I prove a timid friend to truth, I am
afraid that I will not survive to be read by those
to whom these times are ancient.

—Dante

CONTENTS

TIMELINE

𝔍𝔣 𝔊𝔬𝔡 𝔰𝔭𝔞𝔯𝔢 𝔪𝔶 𝔩𝔦𝔣𝔢, 𝔢𝔯𝔢 𝔪𝔞𝔫𝔶 𝔶𝔢𝔞𝔯𝔰 𝔍 𝔴𝔦𝔩𝔩 𝔠𝔞𝔲𝔰𝔢 𝔞 𝔟𝔬𝔶 𝔱𝔥𝔞𝔱 𝔡𝔯𝔦𝔳𝔢𝔱𝔥 𝔱𝔥𝔢 𝔭𝔩𝔬𝔲𝔤𝔥 𝔰𝔥𝔞𝔩𝔩 𝔨𝔫𝔬𝔴 𝔪𝔬𝔯𝔢 𝔬𝔣 𝔱𝔥𝔢 𝔰𝔠𝔯𝔦𝔭𝔱𝔲𝔯𝔢 𝔱𝔥𝔞𝔫 𝔱𝔥𝔬𝔲 𝔡𝔬𝔰𝔱.

—WILLIAM TYNDALE, TO GLOUCESTERSHIRE CLERIC

1381–84: John Wycliffe translates the Bible into English from Latin.

1408: The Constitutions of Oxford forbid any English translation of the Bible.

1455: Johannes Gutenberg prints the first book, the Bible, with movable type.

1494: William Tyndale is born in Gloucestershire.

1505–6: Tyndale begins studies at Oxford.

1512: Tyndale receives a bachelor's degree at Oxford. He privately studies and teaches scripture.

1515: Tyndale receives a master's degree at Oxford. Thomas Wolsey is appointed lord chancellor of England.

1516: Erasmus publishes a Greek edition of the New Testament.

1517: Martin Luther launches the Reformation in Wittenberg, Germany.

1517–21: To further his scholarship, Tyndale moves to Cambridge, where he makes friends with future martyrs.

1521–23: Tyndale takes a job as a tutor in Little Sodbury, where is he accused of heresy. He determines to translate the Bible into English.

1524: Tyndale travels to London and meets Humphrey Monmouth. He seeks permission from Bishop Tunstall to translate.

1524–25: Tyndale goes into self-exile on the Continent. He flees to Cologne, Germany, with printed portions of his New Testament.

1526: Tyndale prints his first New Testament in Worms and begins smuggling books into England. His translation is banned and burned in England.

1527: English agents begin looking for Tyndale on the Continent.

1528: Tyndale publishes *The Parable of the Wicked Mammon* and *The Obedience of a Christian Man.*

1529: Sir Thomas More becomes lord chancellor of England. More publishes his *Dialogue Concerning Heresies,* attacking Tyndale. Tyndale suffers a shipwreck, losing his translations and books.

1530: John Stokesley becomes bishop of London. Thomas Hitton is burned at the stake. Tyndale publishes the Pentateuch.

1531: Thomas Bilney and Richard Bayfield are burned at the stake. Thomas Cromwell becomes a powerful influence in the English court. Stephen Vaughan promises Tyndale safe conduct to England. Tyndale writes *An Answer to Sir Thomas More's Dialogue.*

1532: James Bainham is burned at the stake. Thomas More writes his *Confutation,* but Tyndale refuses to reply.

1533: Thomas Cranmer is appointed archbishop of Canterbury. Anne Boleyn is crowned queen of England. Tyndale's dearest friend, John Frith, is burned at the stake.

1534: Tyndale publishes his revised New Testament and the book of Genesis. He moves into Thomas Poyntz's house in Antwerp.

1535: Tyndale is betrayed by Henry Phillips and arrested. Miles Coverdale publishes the entire Bible in English. Sir Thomas More is beheaded for treason.

1536: William Tyndale is strangled and burned at the stake in Brussels.

1537: John Rogers publishes Matthew's Bible.

1539: Henry VIII allows the Great Bible in every parish church in England. Thomas Cromwell is executed.

1611: The King James Bible is published.

PREFACE

The nature of God's word is, that whosoever read it, or hear it reasoned and disputed before him, it will begin immediately to make him every day better and better, till he be grown into a perfect man.

—WILLIAM TYNDALE, "PROLOGUE UPON THE GOSPEL OF ST. MATTHEW"

THE FORGOTTEN APOSTLE

Several tourists were standing before the stone faces of Mt. Rushmore when someone asked, "Who are those guys anyway?" A shocked silence greeted the inquiry before someone answered, "They are the faces of America's greatest presidents."

It seems inconceivable that anyone would fail to know the contributions of Washington, Jefferson, Lincoln, or Roosevelt. Yet if there were a Mt. Rushmore of the Restoration, would people consider it strange to see the face of William Tyndale alongside the faces of Joseph Smith, Hyrum Smith, and Brigham Young? Next to those latter-day prophets, surely no individual did more to prepare the way for the Restoration than William Tyndale. And though many biographies trace his life, he remains relatively unknown to Latter-day Saints.

The opposition marshaled against him was mountainous. From the brilliant Sir Thomas More to King Henry VIII, from Charles V to the pope, the leading personalities of his century drew upon all of their resources to stop him. At a time when religious authorities condemned heretics to death by fire, church and state hunted him relentlessly. More than a thousand years of cruelty, intolerance, and ignorance barred his way, but the candle in his soul kindled a light sufficient to bring tens of millions to their Savior.

With mustard-seed faith, William Tyndale laid a critical foundation stone of the Restoration. His victory came shortly after his martyrdom, but by then he had fought many a battle that Joseph Smith would not need to wage.

His name floats like a vague memory, his story unfamiliar, but without him and those few who fought the desperate conflict with him, the black shadow of apostasy might still darken the world. He is the unknown disciple, the forgotten apostle, the father of the Testaments, the creator of the prophetic and apostolic voice, the Elias of the European wilderness whose persistent cry finally triumphed and placed in our hands the bread of heaven, the manna of the Word.

This is his story.

SHOEMAKERS
AND WIDOWS

It has long been my cherished wish to cleanse the Lord's temple of barbarous ignorance, and to adorn it with treasures brought from afar, such as may kindle in generous hearts a warm love for the Scriptures.

—ERASMUS OF ROTTERDAM, *ENCHIRIDION MILITIS CHRISTIANI*

A SPRING DAY IN COVENTRY

It was a spring day, not unlike any other April morning, but for seven parents this would be their last. Six men and one woman walked in procession to the Little Park, where stakes were set in the ground. Bundles of straw and sticks lay piled nearby. Today, seven would face the heretic's fire. They were ordinary people who could have lived in a hundred different hamlets of England. Their names are preserved, though none of them lived a life worthy of the historian's pen: "Mistress Smith, Widow; Robert Hatchets, a Shoemaker; Archer, a Shoemaker; Hawkins, a Shoemaker; Thomas Bond, a Shoemaker; Wrigsham, a Glover; Landsdale, a Hosier, martyred at Coventry."

The entry is brief. What crime demanded the torments of such a desperate end? The old document answers: "The principal cause of the apprehension of these persons, was for teaching their children and family the Lord's Prayer and Ten Commandments in English."[1]

Their frightened children, forced to provide evidence against them, recited what they had been taught.

I

Our Father who art in Heaven . . .

Out of the mouths of babes came the damaging testimony to light the fires of Coventry.

Hallowed be thy name . . .

With each new English phrase, the clerics' persecuting zeal flamed higher, fanned by the simple words that rolled from the children's lips.

Give us this day our daily bread . . .

Their parents had been caught earlier and forced to carry a bundle of sticks, reeds, and straw as a warning that scripture was not to be translated into the common English tongue.

And forgive us our debts, as we forgive our debtors . . .

They were relapsed heretics, obstinately refusing to heed the law of God's holy church.

And lead us not into temptation . . .

The tear-filled voices continued, urged on by their inquisitors.

But deliver us from evil . . .

There was little hope of last-minute mercy.

For thine is the kingdom . . .

Sin worthy of death had been committed. All that remained was the final *Amen.*

Only the Widow Smith received a reprieve. She was dismissed and sent on her way. Unhappily for her, the examination lingered till dusk, when Simon Mourton, the bishop's summoner, offered to escort her home in the gathering dark. Taking her arm, he heard the rustle of papers in her long sleeve.

"What have ye here?" he asked, pulling a precious roll from its hiding place. The Ten Commandments and the Lord's Prayer greeted his eyes, but the words from Sinai did not appear in the lofty Latin of the centuries but rather in the vulgar English. "Come, as good now as another time," he said, and he returned her to the bishop, who condemned her with the six men sentenced earlier.[2]

And so they were burned. Their children were warned to forget the offending words placed in their memory by loving parents and

The martyrs of Coventry.

to remember only the fate they had suffered. The same fate awaited them if they ever again dared to compromise God's word by reducing it to their mother tongue.

THE RUSTLE OF A TURNING PAGE

It is hard for us today, with our Bible comfortably resting in the fold of our hands, to understand the sacrifices required to bring it out of the darkness of an earlier age to the light of modern eyes. We ponder in shock that a standard question of the Inquisition was, "Have you read or do you own the scriptures in the common tongue?"

We hear the familiar rustle of a turning page, we read the beautifully crafted words, we feel the emotion created by the rhythmic cadence of oft-repeated lines, we discuss the meaning of parables, and we stand in awe at the Savior's mercy. We teach our families of Jonah and a great fish, of Jacob's love for Rachel and Ruth's love for Naomi, and of the good Samaritan, the prodigal son, and the Sermon on the Mount. We hear the words of Jesus and picture him walking on the Sea of Galilee, feeding five thousand with a few barley loaves, and cleansing the temple of the money changers. We follow Paul from Athens to Corinth to Ephesus and read letters penned to beloved converts. Reading sacred writ is as easy as setting a table, walking a dog, or smelling a flower in the backyard.

With our Bible resting on our lamp stands and bookshelves, do we ever wonder if our own courage equals that of shoemakers and widows? And if not, are we sufficiently grateful for the ease with which we reach for divine truth? Do we realize the faith demanded of former souls whose hunger for the harvest of God's words cleared the forests of resistance, dug out the stumps, piled the rocks, and turned the hard soil so that the seed of the word might be planted in fertile minds?

A FIRE IN THE BONES

We do not know the exact English words the children spoke to the friars of Coventry. The man who put the beautiful Lord's Prayer into the English of the King James Bible had not yet discovered his life's calling. But he was being prepared. The heretic's fire could only be equaled by another fiercely burning fire, and God lit such a fire in the bones of a man named William Tyndale.

When Jeremiah was arrested for preaching in Jerusalem, he was placed in the stocks as punishment. In his misery he told the Lord he was through with calling his generation to repentance. Could God not see what they did to him? But as he sat there, a public spectacle for the mocking scorn of his fellow citizens, he realized that God's word had a power greater than all the hostility mustered against it. "His word was in mine heart," Jeremiah wrote, "as a burning fire shut up in my bones, and I was weary with forbearing, and I could not stay" (Jeremiah 20:9).

A few years ago in Little Sodbury, England, I stood behind a small wooden pulpit—the one used by young William Tyndale in his early years when the voice of God began to stir within him—and I felt a spiritual tug of holiness. Great deeds had been done for future generations and must not be forgotten. I sat in the old scarred chairs of the dining hall in the Walsh Manor and reflected on my own love for the two great Testaments. In the upstairs bedroom where Tyndale studied and prayed, the hallowed words I first heard as a boy from my mother's lips drifted through my mind with the casual ease of beloved friends, and the warmth poured in. Here the great vision was born in his soul. Here God kindled the fire in his bones, knowing that a boy prophet, who would not be born for three centuries, would need the gracious words of James.

As I traveled to Oxford, London, Cologne, and Worms—the stopping places on the road to William Tyndale's own inevitable Carthage—I felt a certain blush of soul that Tyndale had not been part of my conscious memory. For many years I had been lifted and inspired by the voices he gave to prophets and apostles and to Jesus himself, and yet, he stood unacknowledged in the tablets of my mind. His life is still shrouded in the mist of secrecy in which he moved while he lived, always one step ahead of the heresy hunters until he had safely captured the sacred words in the black ink of the printer's craft, words that cried out to echo in English ears.

GREATER THAN THE GREATEST FICTION

The English language was gifted with two men of genius: William Shakespeare and William Tyndale. Shakespeare's bell has tolled across the landscape of history, his name a portrait boldly hanging on the wall of our memory. He penned timeless phrases such as *tongue-tied, green-eyed jealousy, the crack of doom, without rhyme or reason, to budge an inch, laughingstock, slept not a wink, the long and short of it, leapfrog,* and hundreds of other everyday phrases that slip easily from our lips.

Tyndale's bell tower stands silent, the rope slack, the bell ringer asleep, and yet, not even Shakespeare's influence has been so broad or his words read more lovingly. What a carillon would sound if we realized the spoken word of faith and the dialect of belief we owe to William Tyndale.

Atonement, Jehovah, mercy seat, the still small voice, let there be light, in my Father's house are many mansions, a man after his own heart, with God all things are possible, be not weary in well doing, the powers that be, I stand at the door and knock, and *eat, drink and be merry* are all Tyndale's creations. He gave them birth; time has nursed them to maturity.

Tyndale's life reads like a novel of greater fact than fiction could imagine. It is filled with heroes and villains, secrecy, exile, loving friends, and scheming betrayers. He knew the smugglers' secret marks and their intense fraternal loyalty. He tasted the salt of shipwreck and braved the despair of lost manuscripts buried under the waves. Intrigue, safe houses, bribes, spies, covert conversations, drunken apprentices speaking too freely into eager ears, aliases, last-minute flight, imprisonment, and loneliness all wove their spell into the riddles of his hidden world. He drew Henry VIII, Anne Boleyn, Sir Thomas More, Thomas Cromwell, Martin Luther, and Cardinal Thomas Wolsey into the magnetic circle of the intensity of his belief.

Enemies went to all ends to stop him; friends went to the stake for his cause.

Hailed as a saint and condemned to the blackest pit of hell, William Tyndale lived in a world-changing time, a world of whispers and shouts. He altered that world more than any of his contemporaries, and in doing so he brought all of us closer to God.

NOTES

1. Foxe, *Acts and Monuments,* 4:557.
2. Ibid.

"OF GREAT WORTH UNTO THE GENTILES"

To keep us from knowledge of the truth, they do all things in Latin. They pray in Latin, they christen in Latin, they bless in Latin, they give absolution in Latin, only curse they in the English tongue.

—WILLIAM TYNDALE, *THE OBEDIENCE OF A CHRISTIAN MAN*

LOOK!

In God's panoramic vision of the history of the earth, some significant events have been singled out for seers' eyes to preview and prophetic pens to record. Nephi saw *and* recorded such events. With his father's dream stirring in his heart, young Nephi drew aside into quiet solitude and "was caught away in the Spirit of the Lord." There in a place Nephi "never had before seen," the Lord unfolded to his eyes the dramatic prologue to the Restoration, which Isaiah called "a marvellous work and a wonder" (1 Nephi 11:1; Isaiah 29:14).

Three great preparatory events dominated Nephi's vision. "Look!" the angel instructed, and Nephi saw three Spanish caravels tossed courageously across the Atlantic to land on unknown shores. The world proved much more vast than the sea-weary mariners fathomed. Their advancing footsteps, quickly washed smooth by the rising tides, foreshadowed the conquest and civilizing of two continents. The host land for the rolling back of the Apostasy's centuries-old dark curtain loomed out of the ocean waves, a new haven for the old world's captive spirits.

"Look!" and Nephi saw ocean currents alive with tall-masted ships whose immigrant cargo would push inland along trails beaten smooth by bare or moccasin-covered feet. Forest paths soon widened to roads, dotted with villages and then cities as the unforgiving desire for tame land drove Lamanite children of the wilderness farther from the swath of the Gentiles' prophetic advance. But conflict with "mother Gentiles" focused Nephi's vision as battles "upon the waters, and upon the land" resulted in the formation of a new dominion, one "delivered by the power of God out of the hands of all other nations" (1 Nephi 13:17–19). The freshly plowed seedbed soon yielded the fruits of freedom granted by God and enumerated in Jefferson's Declaration and Madison's child, the Constitution.

The fertile land brought forth a young nation that awaited a boy's prayer to consecrate its destiny. That boy would read James's words by candlelight and ponder them under sunlight as his calloused hands gripped a plow and swung an ax. But before the apostolic promise of God's wisdom could germinate the seeds of the Restoration, before the mother Gentiles could be vanquished in the battle for freedom, before multitudes could sail forth out of captivity toward the promised land, a final preparatory pillar remained to be set.

For centuries of apostate night, James's apostolic promise that God would give to any that lacked wisdom, as recorded in the stately rhythms of the English language, was hidden from the unlearned man. The apostle's moving words were locked in the coffin of a dead language. The scholar's Latin sealed the divine truths in quiet darkness.

A Book Carried Forth among Them

"I beheld a book, and it was carried forth among them" (1 Nephi 13:20). With such a simple phrase, one of the great miracles of the latter days was introduced, an event worthy of sharing company with the discovery of the Americas and the triumph of the American experience. Nephi saw the Bible in the hands of the common man. Stern, old pilgrim fathers who effortlessly read the old familiar stories from generation to generation found comfort and wisdom from ancient friends, mercy from the Good Shepherd, guidance from the apostolic epistles.

But for centuries the voices of the scriptures had been hushed. Known only in the cloistered halls of monastery, abbey, or university, they were long forbidden in the cottage. Removing plain and precious truth was not the unique problem of darker ages; the very book itself had been removed. It would take the blood of martyrs before the subtle tones and warm music of holy writ could sound joyfully in the ear without the fearful knocking at the door by the fisted hand of arresting authority, before the doctrines of eternal life could enter the casual observations of an evening's table talk without the terror of facing the searing pain of the heretic's fire.

The same spirit that wrought upon Columbus moved the soul of an English youth and set him on a path that gave English voice to Moses, Jesus, and Paul. Nephi saw *two* books of the Restoration, dual testimonies of Jesus. But before Joseph Smith's world-changing translation of the Book of Mormon emerged from frontier America, William Tyndale gave us the English Bible from his self-imposed exile in the bustling publishing centers of Europe. Both gifts cost the giver his life.

Tools to Forge the Iron Rod

Tyndale needed tools to forge the iron rod so that God's children might catch hold of the wisdom of the prophets. He needed the rich, rugged ore of words and the guiding influence of the Spirit. There in the heat of his mind, God's gift through the Holy Ghost could fan the fire of creative inspiration and generate melodiously formed phrases that would sing their way through human memory and settle into the holding places of the heart.

Four hundred years after Christ, the Anglo-Saxons invaded an island separated from the mainland of Europe that would take its name from them—England. Within two hundred years their language had replaced the Celtic tongue, which left no enduring stamp on emerging English other than familiar place names like Thames, Kent, and Salisbury.

A softer invasion was approaching in cowls, not armor. In 597 Pope Gregory sent Christian missionaries led by Augustine. They brought the Latin of the church, and the linguistic vein that Tyndale would mine thickened and swelled in the rising mountain of English speech. Mingling with the common people, the monks and priests blessed the island vocabulary with a host of new words: *apostle, candle, altar, benediction, multiply, seminary, scripture, priest, sacred,* and *amen.*

At the closing of the eighth century, the Scandinavians arrived in raiding parties along the east and south coasts. Their rule was short-lived, but when the last Viking ships sailed east they left a treasury of words that enriched the language: *sky, skin, fellow, dream, birth, window, they, their, them, egg,* and *bull.*

The winds of conflict were gathering across the channel, and the island would soon hear the warm tones of Norman French blowing through every hamlet. William the Conqueror landed his forces, and at Hastings in 1066 he triumphed. The resultant Norman victory eventually graced the language with an influx of French words, creating multiple synonyms for similar actions and objects: *crown, parliament, jury, verdict, painting, souvenir, confession, heresy, virtue, mercy, humble,* and *chapel.*

More than half of modern English traces its roots to the contributions of Latin and French.[1]

REFINING THE ORE

As vocabulary grew, word order changed. By the 1500s (Tyndale's generation), the English had developed a love affair with their language. They viewed language as today's industrialized world views electronic technology. New words were created by the thousands.

English became the most fertile, colorful, robust, and splendid language on earth. Tyndale had the luxury of selecting from a vast array of sounds, fitting together a wide variety of words, and exploring for subtle distinctions of meaning until the music of scripture sang its way into the soul, creating love for its truths and a desire to live them.

He could select *covenant, bond, testament, oath, vow,* or *promise* as each fit the context. *Holy, blessed, consecrated, hallowed, pure, sacred,* or *sanctified* provided unique shades of meaning and blends of sound. English synonyms created flexibility of expression, allowing a word like *doctrine* to be replaced with *faith, tenet, belief, creed, teaching, principle, rule, law, precept,* or *dogma.*

The English tongue had become a mother lode of expression, rich and ready for Tyndale to mine and mold into Lehi's iron rod—the word of God needed to come before Nephite voices could be forged to blend with their biblical counterparts. Together they would become strong enough for all to hold to and bright enough to part every mist of darkness.

NOTE

1. Word roots come from the *World Book Dictionary* 1:23–25 and from Webster's *Word Histories.*

"I HAVE SEEN THOSE MARTYRS"

𝔍 saw under the altar the souls of them that were killed for the word of God, and they cried with a loud voice, saying How long. . . . And long white garments were given unto every one of them. And it was said unto them that they should rest for a little season until the number of their fellows, and brethren, and of them that should be killed as they were, were fulfilled.

—WILLIAM TYNDALE, REVELATION 6:9–11 (1526 EDITION)

A BOOK BY JOHN FOXE

𝔍n 1834 the Prophet Joseph Smith visited the small Church branch at Pontiac, Michigan. As during all of his travels, throngs desired to hear the man who translated the Mormon "Golden Bible." Standing at a table, which served as a pulpit, Joseph held the assembly of farmers and tradesmen with the voice of conviction as he boldly related the visit of the Father and the Son at the dawn of the Restoration. Few were baptized, but Edward Stevenson did not doubt the truthfulness of the speaker. He received the Prophet into his home and offered him a present of "some of our choice apples." But Edward's house held sweeter treasure than Michigan apples. That treasure—a copy of John Foxe's *Book of Martyrs*—caught the Prophet's eye. Edward later described Joseph's reaction:

"He expressed sympathy for the Christian martyrs and a hope for their salvation. He asked to borrow the book, promising to return it when he should meet us again in Missouri. On returning

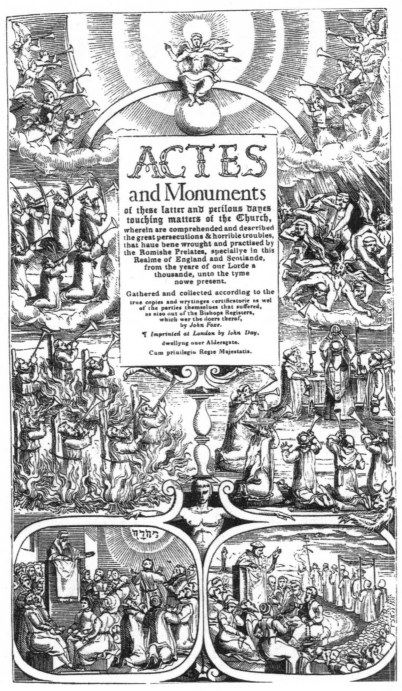

John Foxe's Actes and Monuments.

it he said, 'I have, by the aid of the Urim and Thummim, seen those martyrs. They were honest, devoted followers of Christ, according to the light they possessed. They will be saved."[1]

Perhaps Joseph felt a foreshadowing of his own death in the martyred sufferings of the early Saints and reformers. He certainly had reason to believe martyrdom was coming; early hints of his fate appeared in revelations published in the Doctrine and Covenants. The Lord had told him, "Be firm in keeping the commandments . . . and if you do this, behold I grant unto you eternal life, even if you should be slain. . . . For they can do no more unto you than unto me. And even if they do unto you even as they have done unto me, blessed are ye, for you shall dwell with me in glory" (D&C 5:22; 6:29–30).

What were Joseph's thoughts as he turned the pages, reading sorrowful tales of imprisonment, torture, and the stake, and pondering the courageous testimonies that held firm to the last painful leap of the flames? As the wheels jolted in the ruts of the frontier road, was Joseph's mind captured by compelling stories whose details harmonized with his own experience?

A Shadow of His Own Life

In time the Prophet would come to a chapter titled "The Life and Story of the True Servant and Martyr of God, William Tyndale." This chapter contained shadows of Joseph's own life, down to Tyndale's final prayer at the release of death. Like Joseph, William had been given the gift of translation, the spiritual endowment called "the interpretation of tongues." Both men were hounded and driven from place to place. Both were sensitive, trusting, guileless, and susceptible to the weak or false friend. Both never knew the security of a permanent home or the ambience of abiding peace. Both died at an early age. Both were betrayed, imprisoned, and killed—Joseph by the bullets of an enraged mob, William by strangulation and fire in a public square. Both were killed by self-satisfied men representing the condemnation of church or state.

Yet both men had experienced the sacrificing loyalty of friends and the deep satisfaction of knowing that God was pleased with their offering. Both knew their work would endure, for they gave humanity priceless gifts. One produced the Book of Mormon, the other the English Bible—twin testimonies of God's redeeming Son. The enduring publication of these books—heaven's best-sellers—continues to dominate the publishing world.

The wagon bumped and jolted along while Joseph turned the pages. Finally, filled with a curiosity born of the persecution in his own life, he turned his eyes in a quiet moment to the revelatory tool God had given him and asked of the martyrs' fate. A merciful God responded, allowing the Prophet to see those who had gone before him. "They were honest, devoted followers of Christ. . . . They will be saved."

William Tyndale, for his honesty, devotion, and sacrifice, will be among them.

NOTE

1. Andrus, *They Knew the Prophet,* 85.

"GOD'S MATTOCK TO SHAKE THE FOUNDATION"

𝕲𝔬𝔡, for a secret judgment and purpose, and for his godly pleasure, provided an hour that thy father and mother should come together, to make thee through them. 𝕳e was present with thee in thy mother's womb and fashioned thee and breathed life into thee, and for the great love he had unto thee moved also thy father and mother and all others to love thee, to pity thee, and to care for thee.

—WILLIAM TYNDALE, *THE OBEDIENCE OF A CHRISTIAN MAN*

THE FLINT THAT BEGAT THE SPARK

In *Foxe's Book of Martyrs,* William Tyndale is introduced "as God's mattock to shake the inward roots and foundation" of a Christian world dominated by Catholic Rome.[1] Little is known of his youth, but one intriguing story, related by Tyndale himself, seems to indicate that the fire in his bones that compelled him toward the martyr's stake was struck in his childhood. The tale of an ancient English king provided the flint.

"Except my memory fail me, and that I have forgotten what I read when I was a child, thou shalt find in the English chronicle, how that king Athelstane caused the holy scripture to be translated into the tongue that then was in England, and how the prelates [abbots or bishops] exhorted him thereto,"[2] he wrote.

The place of his birth and the names of his parents are unknown, and records of his life before Oxford do not exist. But William's brother Edward, a man of influence, lived for thirty years

19

in a house called Hurst Farm, located roughly a mile from the village of Slimbridge in Gloucestershire. The best evidence suggests that William was born here in 1494, two years after Columbus's historic voyage. His family also went by the name Hutchins.[3] According to a tradition recorded in a 1663 letter by a descendant of Edward, the first Tyndale was of northern origin, a Yorkish loyalist who fled south during the Wars of the Roses and changed his name as a protection. Only on his deathbed did he reveal to his children his true identity. Mystery and intrigue, it seems, flowed in William's blood.

"ABOUT THE BORDERS OF WALES"

William Tyndale was "born about the borders of Wales."[4] Overlooking the small village of North Nibley is Nibley Knoll, upon which a monument to the great translator has been built. From the top of its tower, the eye takes in numerous counties stretching into a hazy green distance of patchwork. To the east lies the Cotswold Hills. To the west the Severn River flows through the Vale of Berkeley. The Castle of Berkeley, where Edward II was murdered and William the Conqueror was crowned, excites the mind with images of proud monarchs and trailing companies of mailed knights, bright banners flying in the breeze. Perhaps these memories infused young William with a wonder of old English kings that kindled in him Athelstane's desire to see the Bible in the mother tongue.

The Tyndale family was blessed with sufficient wealth to secure positions of trust and live comfortably. William received a formal university education. His brother John bought and sold wool with the merchants of London. Among these merchants William would find smuggling partners to bring his Bibles past the vigilant eyes of church and state. He was intelligent, active, inquisitive, and confident enough to challenge the authorities of the day early in his life. He, like Joseph Smith, was "destined to prove a disturber and an annoyer" of the adversary's kingdom from his youth (Joseph Smith–History 1:20). The one constant in William's young life was the desire that farmers, milkmaids, and other commoners who worked in the villages of his homeland know the scriptural narratives his own Latin education had allowed him to read and ponder.

WYCLIFFE AND THE LOLLARDS

Gloucestershire was fertile ground for Tyndale's inclinations. In an earlier century, John Wycliffe had struck the first blow against apostasy's grip in England by sending out itinerant preachers—"poor priests" or "true men" armed with manuscript translations of the Bible. They shared these translations in taverns, village greens, forests, and private homes with all who dared to listen. Because manuscripts were costly and time-consuming to produce, many of Wycliffe's followers traveled with a single gospel, committing whole books to memory to partially escape the prohibitions of the law.

In the twilight, after the day's work was done, the blacksmiths and coopers gathered by the flicker of a candle or the glow of a hearth to hear the prized words recalled from memory or read from tattered parchments until too frequent readings turned the rag paper to dust. Many of those caught preaching scripture in the mother tongue were burned with the offending translations hung around their necks, tall conical hats perched mockingly on their heads. The crime of butchers and weavers reading Christ's words was fought with strenuous punishments, but Wycliffe had brought light into a religious world that preferred the obscurity of concealing darkness.

Nicknamed "Lollards" after the old German word *lollen*, which means to mutter or hum, Wycliffe's movement was driven underground. His bones were exhumed after his death, publicly burned for heresy, and then scattered on the River Swift so no remaining ash could be gathered to preserve his memory. But he was remembered! Lollards persisted during Tyndale's youth because thirst for the scriptures had not abated since the time of Wycliffe. Cottagers still assembled in secret to hear the precious word even if only a few pages of a gospel or epistle were available. They risked their lives doing so, but the word of God was worth it.

FOLK WISDOM OF THE COMMON MAN

Tyndale received something more from the Vale of Berkeley than a hunger for the English word. His ear grew tuned to the ancient mastery of the common people to enshrine wisdom in short, trenchant phrases. He drew in with the air he breathed the flow and rhythm of everyday speech without any affectation. Because the Savior, who chose disciples from the fishermen of Galilee and crafted his own wisdom to match the thirst of simple souls, was a master of this teaching style, Tyndale was prepared to give voice to the Son of God. His translations yield myriad examples: "strait is the gate, and narrow is the way," "signs of the times," "seek and ye shall find," "the salt of the earth," "the spirit is willing, but the flesh is weak," and "no man can serve two masters."[5]

Scriptural language has a lift, a certain musical quality that heightens its effect. This lift adds an endorsement of truth, a kind of testimony inherent in the words and phrases themselves. We find that testimony most often in simple, monosyllabic combinations of words. Those who love God's truth produce endorsements of it with such phrases as, "It was meet that we should make merry, and be glad: for this thy brother was dead, and is alive again; and was lost, and is found."[6]

Tyndale's translation of Jesus' words to his disciples when his "hour" had come provide another example: "Peace I leave with you, my peace I give unto you: not as the world giveth, give I unto you." The deeply moving prayer from Gethsemane is also from Tyndale: "O my Father, if it be possible, let this cup pass from me: nevertheless not as I will, but as thou wilt." Christ's comforting words at the Last Supper as rendered by Tyndale also illustrate a spiritual lift: "In my Father's house are many mansions: if it were not so, I would have told you. I go to prepare a place for you" (John 14:27; Matthew 26:39; John 14:2).[7]

Other versions of the Bible reveal the loss of this spiritual lift. Somehow, "There are many rooms in my Father's house" (Jerusalem Bible and the New International Version) or "There are many homes up there where my Father lives" (Living Bible) just do not match the majesty of Tyndale nor of the Redeemer, who first made the comforting promise. Joseph Smith rightly keeps Tyndale's "mansions" when choosing his own wording in Enos and Moroni (Enos 1:27; Ether 12:37).

Tyndale's gift with words was refined by his years at Oxford and Cambridge and by his growing mastery of living and dead languages, yet he remained faithful to the everyday speech he knew as a child. For that reason his words ring true among all classes in every English-speaking country. This is all the more remarkable because English dialects changed from county to county, even in his lifetime, and English was considered backward and rude. Tyndale, however, sensed its power and gave us the voice of Jesus that has found such a profound place in our hearts. He captured the soul and mind of the Master that still sounds right, holy, and understandable five centuries later.

Tyndale's ear for putting the right sounds together crossed over into everyday speech as Britain and her world-encircling colonies became essentially "the people of the book." English at the time was like wet paint applied to the canvas of a masterpiece, with Tyndale wielding the brush. It dried with his brush strokes set in beautiful harmony and color. We have all been speaking "Tyndale" from our infancy. Joseph Smith took that tradition into the Book of Mormon and the Doctrine and Covenants, rendering those modern scriptures equally powerful in their ability to move the heart, activate the mind, and mold character.

NOTES

1. Foxe, *Book of Martyrs,* 176.
2. Mozley, *William Tyndale,* 8–9.
3. Spelled Hychyns and Hewchyns in some sources but standardized here as Hutchins.
4. Foxe, *Acts and Monuments,* 5:114.
5. Daniell, *William Tyndale,* 29, 42, 25, 57, 29; all quotations come from Tyndale's 1534 New Testament.
6. Ibid., 117.
7. Ibid., 155, 57, 154.

JULY 4, 1512 AND JULY 2, 1515
OXFORD, ENGLAND

"SINGULARLY ADDICTED"

We be all equally created and formed of one God our Father, and indifferently bought and redeemed with one blood of our Saviour Jesus Christ. Which two points, I say, if they be written in thine heart, are the keys which so open all the scripture unto thee, that no creature can lock thee out, and with which thou shalt go in and out, and find pasture and food everywhere. And if these lessons be not written in thine heart, then is all the scripture shut up as a kernel in the shell, so that thou mayest read it, and commune of it, and rehearse all the stories of it, and dispute wittily, and be a profound sophistry, and yet understand not one jot thereof.

—WILLIAM TYNDALE, "PROLOGUE TO THE PROPHET JONAS"

BROUGHT UP FROM A CHILD

The continued refining of Tyndale's skills found ample heat in the furnace of Oxford to which he went while still a child. Foxe gives us a brief account of Tyndale's next stage of preparation:

"Brought up from a child in the university of Oxford, where he, by long continuance, grew up, and increased as well in the knowledge of tongues, and other liberal arts, as *especially in the knowledge of the Scriptures, whereunto his mind was singularly addicted;* insomuch that he, lying then in Magdalen hall, *read privily to certain students and fellows of Magdalen college, some parcel of divinity; instructing them in the knowledge and truth of the Scriptures.*"[1]

25

Foxe's description, though ordinary, is remarkable considering the attitudes and curriculum of the English universities of the day. Scholars of the sixteenth century felt it was desirable to instill in young minds the sophistries of the day, especially in religion. Developing intellects were susceptible to the imprints of learned men, but William Tyndale's mind was soft to the stamp of ancient thought, not the scholastics of the university, which he rejected. His academic interests left him alone in the scholarly world for the seven years it took to earn a bachelor's degree at Oxford. During those years, he grew in language, liberal arts, and scripture—skills he would draw on to accomplish his life's work.

The first recorded entry of William's life is July 4, 1512. On that day he received his bachelor of arts under the name William Hychyns. He received his master of arts three years later, on July 2, 1515. Statutes at Oxford's Magdalen College mandated that entrants, or "Demies," be at least twelve years of age. William likely left for Oxford at about this age. That he was not overwhelmed at such an early age by his professors shows the quality of his intellect and spirit.

Before leaving for college, William would have studied Latin, the required language for any serious education, in a local grammar school in Gloucestershire. Indeed, the idea that significant writing could be done in English was simply not entertained. Spoken English was not allowed except on isolated holidays. At the time, England was a backwater country, its language considered rustic and coarse.

Most students entered the university in their mid to late teens. By entering at an earlier age, William showed promise as a scholar. But he was not the only prodigy. A butcher's son who became Cardinal Thomas Wolsey, Lord Chancellor of England under Henry VIII, earned his bachelor's degree from Magdalen College at age fifteen.[2] Wolsey would become Tyndale's enemy and hunt him throughout Europe. In challenging the religious and political status quo, William also took on the high intellect found in Renaissance England.

Tyndale began his university day by studying from 6 to 9 A.M. After breakfast, he resumed his studies until 11 A.M. Following lunch, he studied until 5 P.M. Students at Oxford were almost always mildly hungry and, in the winter, chilly. Their rooms, heated by fires, were smoke-filled and cold.[3] The realities of student life in William's day give value to Shakespeare's description of "the whining school-boy, with his satchel and shining morning face, creeping like a snail unwillingly to school."[4]

At the university, recitation was a common means of instilling knowledge in young minds, which required reading texts out loud. Vocal reading trained William's ear for the cadences and symmetry of human speech and helped him realize that scripture in particular is enhanced when read out loud. Hearing Virgil's majestic poetry or Cicero's sweeping prose tuned William's ear in a way unfamiliar to academe today but which was critical for the development of his genius, which is best realized when listening to his resonating phrases.

THE RHETORICAL TRADITION

Liberal arts studies centered on the *trivium,* which consisted of grammar, logic, and rhetoric; and on the *quadrivium,* which consisted of arithmetic, music (including poetry), astronomy, and geometry. Students studied Euclid, Ptolemy, Aristotle, Ovid, and Cicero. They graduated with fluency in Latin, a mental keenness for debate, and a mind framed for logic but browbeaten into submission regarding church orthodoxy.

For Tyndale, rhetoric proved useful. Though it has a negative connotation today, rhetoric helped those who mastered its intricacies to fully comprehend the power of words. Well-constructed phrases could persuade, convince, and move the listener. Exercises included rewriting a sentence dozens of ways and examining the effect each rewrite produced. Erasmus' rhetorical manual, *De Copia,* reworked the sentence "Your letter has delighted me very much" 150 different ways.

Clarity of expression was not the only goal. Wisdom and insight were ideally presented in emotive language, which was designed to be pleasurable to hear or read. The enjoyment increased the likelihood that the ideas would be accepted and acted upon. In the non-rhetorical tradition of today, it would be difficult to produce something as magnificent as the King James Bible. English today has largely lost the richness and color of an age that produced Shakespeare. For this reason, the King James Bible remains the preferred edition.

This disciplined rhetorical training heightened Tyndale's sensitivity to the poetic quality of combinations of sounds and stresses. He did not always consciously manipulate words, but as a deeply educated man acting under the guidance of the Holy Spirit, he produced pleasing patterns and sequences. You can hear the whisper of the Holy Spirit in the repetition of the "s" sound and the double "l" in the phrase "still small voice." Latter-day Saints have adopted that phrase as the primary definition of the Holy Ghost, even for children. (Joseph Smith used it in his translation of the Book of Mormon.) We hear the same musical endorsement even in small phrases created by Tyndale such as "mercy seat," which juxtaposes two "s" sounds and fits comfortably in the sacrament song "I Stand All Amazed."[5]

The Lord placed William Tyndale in a tradition and culture best calculated to create the human tools he needed to produce a Bible that would be "of great worth unto the Gentiles" (1 Nephi 13:23). That worth hinged not only on the truth it contained but also on its manner of expression.

THE GIFT OF TONGUES

As late as the early 1600s, the Oxford Library had fewer than one hundred books in English out of its six thousand volumes.[6] But to spark a revolutionary change, Tyndale needed Greek and Hebrew, the original recorded languages of the Bible. Marching ahead of his contemporary scholars, he believed that technical rhetorical skills in Latin could be employed in creating a beautiful Bible in English, which was a perfect medium for catching the grandeur of Hebrew and Greek scripture.

Tyndale was gifted in English as well as in foreign and dead languages. A contemporary wrote that Tyndale was "so skillful in seven tongues . . . that whichever he speaks, you would think it his native tongue."[7] His mastery of languages required effort beyond his Oxford years, but eventually Latin, Greek, Hebrew, Italian, Spanish, French, and German flowed without restraint from his pen and tongue.

Greek was essential because Tyndale drew his translation of the New Testament directly from the Greek text instead of from Jerome's almost worshiped Latin Vulgate—the Latin Bible used by the Catholic Church. The study of Greek was new at Oxford, but when Tyndale left the university, his mastery was such that he translated a difficult piece of classical writing into English in hopes of persuading the bishop of London to employ him for a biblical translation. In time, Tyndale taught himself Hebrew so he could put the wisdom of the Old Testament into English.

"NO MAN SHALL LOOK ON THE SCRIPTURE"

Tyndale's assessment of university education paints an unflattering picture of the dozen or so years he spent there:

"In the universities they have ordained that no man shall look on the scripture, until he be noselled [nurtured] in heathen learning eight or nine years, and armed with false principles; with which he is clean shut out of the understanding of the scripture," he wrote. The student "is sworn that he shall hold none opinion condemned by the church. . . . And then, when they be admitted to study divinity, because the scripture is locked up with such false expositions, and with false principles of natural philosophy, that they cannot enter in, they go about the outside, and dispute all their lives about words and vain opinions."[8]

Tyndale recalls with exasperation some of the debates at Oxford. One centered on the sacramental wafer. Was it still bread considering that the flour "with long lying in water, was turned to starch, and had lost its nature"? He remembered another debate about whether the widow or the virgin had more merit. One had to forgo the joys of marriage after having known them while the other imagined them greater than they were. Who faced the most serious temptations?[9] In light of such discussions, Tyndale preferred his private self-tutorials in the bare text of his Old and New Testaments even though they were in Latin and even though he risked reprimand if caught studying them.

A decade earlier, John Colet had shocked conventional university practice by delivering lectures on Paul's epistles. He restricted himself to the plain text and the simple truths to which Paul testified, but it was as if the apostle had risen from the pages of Romans and Corinthians like a resurrected spirit to walk the halls of Oxford—a breathing, feeling, living human being. Colet attracted huge crowds, testifying to the inherent need for drinking at the source instead of down river. The impact of those moments in the sunlight of pure scripture still reverberated in Oxford's halls, as did whispers about the work of another Oxford scholar—John Wycliffe. Though proscribed and burned, Wycliffe's work continued to circulate in the Christian underground, and the spirit of his sure footsteps and earnest conversations followed Tyndale as he walked the same halls.

OF LIFE UNSPOTTED

In the quiet of his private world at Oxford, William pored over the scriptures by candlelight when he had finished other studies. Yet the spirit to share with others the beautiful truths he loved turned him toward his fellow scholars. Cautiously, choosing with care those to gather around him, he read "privily to certain students and fellows of Magdalen College; instructing them in the knowledge and truth of the Scriptures."[10]

The person Foxe described was not an adult but a boy in his early and late teens. It is hard not to compare the adolescent Tyndale with two other earnest young men who also acquired enough wisdom in their early years to teach others untainted truth—the twelve-year-old Jesus in the temple at Jerusalem and the teenage Joseph Smith in a Palmyra log cabin surrounded by his family.

A man is judged not only by his talent, intellect, and faith but also by his character. This is certainly true if his chosen arena is religion. Fortunately, we have a description, though minimal, of the daily walk of the Father of the English Bible. Foxe concludes in his portrait of Tyndale's Oxford days an entry about his demeanor: "His manners and conversation being correspondent to the same [knowledge and truth of the scriptures], were such, that all they that knew him, reputed and esteemed him to be a man of most virtuous disposition, and of life unspotted."[11]

Foxe, who admired Tyndale, undoubtedly put the best face on his biography. But what of Tyndale's enemies? Sir Thomas More, chancellor of England, became one of Tyndale's fiercest foes, obsessed with destroying him. Yet even he verified Foxe's assessment. Tyndale was "well known," More wrote, "before he went over the sea, for a man of right good living, studious and well learned in scripture, and in divers places in England was very well liked and did great good with preaching."[12] Later in the same work, More added that Tyndale "was indeed . . . taken for a man of sober and honest living, and looked and preached holily."[13]

Hall's Chronicle contained another assessment of Tyndale's virtues: "Such as best knew him reported him to be a very sober man, born about the borders of Wales, and brought up in the University of Oxford and *in life and conversation unreprovable.*"[14]

These qualities proved critical for the selfless work that became William Tyndale's obsession. It is appropriate that the Lord chose such a man. Purity of soul and purpose must accompany the mind that gives voice to apostles and the Son of God. The Spirit, so crucial for Tyndale's work, could not thrive in an unclean temple. Tyndale's early traits prefigure the character of one of the few Reformers who had little to gain from his efforts and everything to risk. His pen could burn hot if occasion required, but it was not his nature to be confrontational. He was the sweet singer of the Reformation, and the man matched the song.

Notes

1. Foxe, *Acts and Monuments,* 5:114–15; emphasis added.
2. Some historians attribute Wolsey's "butcher son" origins to legend, claiming rather that he was the son of a prosperous merchant who could afford to send him to Oxford.
3. Daniell, *William Tyndale,* 25.
4. Shakespeare, *As You Like It,* 2.7.146–48.
5. *Hymns,* no. 193.
6. Daniell, *William Tyndale,* 25.
7. Mozley, *William Tyndale,* 67.
8. Greenslade, *Work of William Tindale,* 153–54.
9. Daniell, *William Tyndale,* 38.
10. Foxe, *Acts and Monuments,* 5:114–15.
11. Ibid., 5:115.
12. More, *Complete Works of St. Thomas More,* 6:28; spelling standardized.
13. Ibid., 6:424; spelling standardized.
14. Hall, *Hall's Chronicle,* 818; emphasis added.

"RIPENED IN THE KNOWLEDGE OF GOD'S WORD"

Remember ye not how within this thirty years and far less . . . the old barking curs . . . the children of darkness, raged in every pulpit against Greek . . . and Hebrew . . . some beating the pulpit with their fists for madness, and roaring out with open and foaming mouth.

—WILLIAM TYNDALE, *An Answer unto Sir Thomas More's Dialogue*

"SPYING HIS TIME"

Sometime between 1517 and 1521, William Tyndale, tired of scholastic games at Oxford and perhaps under suspicion for his emerging views, decided on a change of universities. After earning his master's degree in 1516, he likely taught at Oxford for a year—something that was traditionally required of master's graduates. But once he fulfilled this obligation, Foxe says, he sought another environment more conducive to his scriptural hunger. "Thus he, in the university of Oxford, increasing more and more in learning, and proceeding in degrees of the schools, spying his time, removed from thence to the university of Cambridge."[1]

By "spying his time," Foxe meant that Tyndale made a conscious choice in quitting the university home he had known for more than a decade. Cambridge was a smaller, younger university without the prestige of Oxford, but it was a compelling choice. It offered a quieter setting, one conducive to uninhibited reflection. Overzealous eyes fearful of open examination of scripture would not be as prevalent as at Oxford, whose graduates had a great awareness of events transpiring at their alma mater. Oxford, after all, produced the majority of Tyndale's later persecutors, including Thomas Wolsey, Sir Thomas More, London bishops John Stokesley and Cuthbert Tunstall, and Tyndale's shadowy betrayer, Henry Phillips.

THE CAMBRIDGE MEN OF COURAGE

Undoubtedly, Tyndale learned of growing Lutheran sentiments brewing at Cambridge. In 1517, Luther issued the reformer's challenge by nailing his 95 theses to the Wittenberg church door. The sale of indulgences to finance construction of the massive St. Peter's Basilica in Rome had backfired. The Catholic leadership believed the "uncultured masses" needed "imperishable memorials" highly decorated with art, "something that appeals to the eye" to capture their faith.[2] Tyndale would construct an edifice equal in its magnetic pull to the beauties of Renaissance Italy—a monument that could be held in the hands of the masses.

Luther threw Catholic Europe into a maelstrom that split her into warring factions. For whatever reason, Cambridge attracted the young men who moved the English nation into the Protestant camp. They all paid dearly for their convictions. Bishops Cranmer, Latimer, and Ridley embraced the martyr's stake in Oxford. The place of their burning is still marked to this day. John Frith, one of Tyndale's most beloved followers, as well as Thomas Bilney and Robert Barnes, all early leaders in the Protestant movement, also chose death rather than renounce their faith. Miles Coverdale, who helped Tyndale translate the Old Testament and later saw the entire Bible published in English, also attended Cambridge.

Officially, ideas of reform were discouraged at Cambridge, as they were everywhere else. A public burning of Luther's books in 1520 undoubtedly troubled Tyndale, reminding him that his own ambitions for the "word" would meet stiff opposition. But reform was in the air, and would-be reformers held meetings in an inn called the White Horse, dubbed "Little Germany" because of its liberal gatherings. How often they met and who attended are matters of speculation; nevertheless, many of Tyndale's friends and future fellow martyrs frequented Cambridge and fueled each other's inquiries into the distressing condition of Christianity.

Greeks and Trojans

At Oxford the debate over the influence of Greek became hostile, with two camps, the "Greeks" and the "Trojans," emerging from the fray. At Cambridge the Greeks were winning the war, and the gates of Troy had already let in the Trojan Horse. Tyndale may have preferred Cambridge because he could hone his Greek skills there. In 1516, Erasmus of Rotterdam, one of the most intelligent and gentle souls of the Reformation, published a Greek New Testament, thus offering the religious world an opportunity to read the words of Jesus and Paul more directly than the Latin Vulgate allowed. Improved editions that followed in 1519 and 1522 would become Tyndale's tools.

John Wycliffe's condemned translation had been drawn from the Latin into English; Tyndale wanted to render his New Testament from the purer Greek and his Old Testament from the Hebrew. He was convinced that English could provide a language hearty and beautiful enough to carry the highest thoughts of prophets and apostles. Indeed, it was perfectly suited for the task. But English was still considered an emerging language. Its flexibility and grace for conveying classical and scriptural thought was not only denied but was also, in most minds, not worthy of consideration. In a manner of speaking, Tyndale was a pilgrim in his beliefs, rowing across the Atlantic ahead of the *Mayflower.*

In all likelihood, the unique environment Cambridge offered for deeper searching of God's word created enough reason for Tyndale's move. Foxe agrees that the scriptures were the major focus of Tyndale's sojourn at Cambridge, where he was "further ripened in the knowledge of God's word."[3] He was not interested in another degree, having experienced enough scholasticism at Oxford.

However, sometime in the late Oxford or Cambridge period, he was ordained a priest. He now chose, however, to use his knowledge in teaching rather than in administering the sacramental duties of the parish priest. Returning to Gloucestershire, he became a tutor to the two small sons of Sir John Walsh. There his troubles began.

NOTES

1. Foxe, *Acts and Monuments,* 5:115.
2. Moynahan, *God's Bestseller,* 14.
3. Foxe, *Acts and Monuments,* 5:115.

"IF GOD SPARE MY LIFE"

Now faith . . . is the gift of God, given us by grace. . . . I never deserved it, nor prepared myself unto it; but ran another way clean contrary in my blindness, and sought not that way; but he sought me, and found me out, and showed it me, and therewith drew me to him. And I bow the knees of my heart unto God night and day, that he will show it all other men; and I suffer all that I can, to be a servant to open their eyes. For well I wot they cannot see of themselves.

—WILLIAM TYNDALE, *AN ANSWER UNTO SIR THOMAS MORE'S DIALOGUE*

A TUTOR TO LITTLE BOYS

It was inevitable that a clash with the local clergy would come. Leaving Cambridge, Tyndale returned to his home county of Gloucestershire to the tiny village of Little Sodbury, where he settled into the manor of John Walsh[1] as tutor to John's two sons. What could have been his motive in accepting an unimportant position in a tiny hamlet when his talents could be exercised more prominently? Had he not yet determined his life's work and returned home to contemplate his future? Did he need a recluse to further his studies and preparation?

In Gloucestershire, the resolve to bring the Bible's voice to his countrymen became Tyndale's grand obsession. The stifling life of the university had become distasteful to him, closing off the occupation of lecturer. Scripture was his passion, but teaching or translating it was not welcome at Oxford or Cambridge.

Tyndale was an ordained priest, but this avenue of support was also repugnant to him, especially in light of the contrast between what he learned from scriptural research on the primitive church and current clerical practices. While at Cambridge, he had surely witnessed the 1520 visit of Cardinal Thomas Wolsey and the ceremonial splendor in which he was received, complete with fulsome eulogies and fawning praise. All of this would have excited in Tyndale an already growing mistrust of church leadership. His comfort level in performing the Catholic sacraments, many of which had no foundation in scripture, was an additional hindrance to his assuming the office of a priest. Yet he had to earn his living some way.

It is almost certain that William's brother Edward played a lead role in securing his position at the Walsh manor. Was the position deliberately created to allow Tyndale time to continue his studies with the Greek New Testament? His duties with the manor's little boys were minimal. Little Sodbury provided a quiet environment, free of time-consuming obligations, in a comfortable, supportive atmosphere. Whatever Tyndale's motives were, he moved into an attic room in the Walsh manor.

"If I Preach Not the Gospel"

Tyndale did not quietly retire into a life of teaching occasional grammar or math lessons with free time spent in private pursuits with his books. The knowledge he was gaining from the New Testament needed an outlet. The words of Paul, which Tyndale perused so deeply and frequently, found resonance in his own situation. "Though I preach the gospel, I have nothing to glory of: for necessity is laid upon me; yea, woe is unto me, if I preach not the gospel!" (1 Corinthians 9:16).

The two active poles of Tyndale's life began to augment each other. His knowledge created a desire to share what he was discovering, and the need to edify and feed a scripturally famished population fueled his search for more nourishing truths. But where could he preach? And what danger would it entail?

A small private chapel dedicated to St. Adeline, the patron saint of weavers, stood just a few yards from the manor house. Here was a starting place, but the limited confines of a private family chapel did not give proper scope to Tyndale's expanding desires. Instead, he would soon preach in the open air like the apostles of old and in any venue he could secure. Since the time of the Lollards, preaching was discouraged and dangerous. It was associated with dissent for good reason. In time, preaching became as effective a weapon for Protestants as the printing press. Comparing Tyndale's later preaching in London to his early Little Sodbury forays, Foxe related that he preached "according as he had done in the country before, and especially about the town of Bristol, and also in the said town, in the common place called St. Austin's Green."[2]

Field preachers were not new in England. They offered spiritual edification as well as entertainment, depending on their talents. The "Green" Foxe referred to is a parcel of open ground in front of an old Augustinian convent in Bristol. To reach Bristol, fifteen miles from Little Sodbury, required a healthy walk.

Tyndale's preaching differed in major ways from traditional approaches in that he drew significant portions of his sermons directly from the words of Jesus and the early evangelists. For his listeners, Tyndale's preaching was akin to seeing a distant hazy landscape suddenly brought into view with the persistent fog melting away. It is a fair assumption that he emphasized the saving power of faith in Christ as stressed by Paul—void of the necessity of the confessional, indulgences, relics, appeals to the saints, pilgrimages, or other acts of penance that the clergy insisted upon and from which they received a large portion of their monetary gains. All of this could not have failed to bring Tyndale under the scrutiny and animosity of the local religious establishment, but it was his private dinner conversations at the Walsh table with the clerical dignitaries of the day that broke the camel's back.

SECRET GRUDGES

The table of an English manor, such as the Walsh family kept, included many guests of high standing. Because the church held considerable property, and the bishops, archdeacons, and other church authorities wielded notable ecclesiastical and economic authority, their presence in the Walsh household would be expected and frequent. Yet here they met an upstart young priest, versed in Greek and Latin. What galled them further, he obviously had a better grasp of scriptural truth than they did. A suspiciously heretical twist accompanied his conversation, and he preached in the open so all could note the difference between the clergy's lives and teachings and his own.

Tyndale, though of a gentle disposition, was not retiring, timid, or overawed by authority, and even in this company he let his views be known, which shows the standing this servant-tutor had gained in the eyes Sir John and Lady Walsh. Richard Webb, of Chipping Sodbury, a neighboring village, reminisced about Tyndale's confrontations with the district priesthood.

"This gentleman, as he kept a good ordinary commonly at his table, there resorted to him many times sundry abbots, deans, archdeacons, with divers other doctors, and great beneficed men; who there together, with Master Tyndale sitting at the same table, did use many times to enter communication, and talk of learned men, as of Luther and of Erasmus; also of divers other controversies and questions upon the Scripture," Webb noted.

"Then Master Tyndale, as he was learned and well practised in God's matters, so he spared not to show unto them simply and plainly his judgment in matters, as he thought; and when they at any time did vary from Tyndale in opinions and judgment, he would show them in the book, and lay plainly before them the open and manifest places of the Scriptures, to confute their errors, and confirm his sayings. And thus continued they for a certain season, reasoning and contending together divers and sundry times, till at length they waxed weary, and bare a secret grudge in their hearts against him."[3]

Though Tyndale's adversaries in the Walsh dining hall were "learned," a dearth of true scriptural knowledge existed among those entrusted with the spiritual welfare of the people. They had a basic grasp of the formulas and rituals, but many could not read the Latin they were using. Even the church itself openly acknowledged ignorance in certain theological areas, particularly regarding the New Testament. It is not surprising that Tyndale bested them in table discussions.

A church survey conducted in Gloucestershire in 1551 by Bishop Hooper discovered that of 311 clerics, nine did not know how many commandments God gave to Moses on Sinai, 33 did not know where to find them in the Bible, 168 could not repeat them, 39 did not know where to find the Lord's Prayer in the New Testament, 34 did not know the author of the prayer, and 10 could not even recite it. In 1560, the London diocese prohibited 22 out of 56 clerics from practicing because of their ignorance.[4]

Tyndale was frank and guileless. It probably never crossed his young mind that older well-positioned men might not take his corrections kindly, no matter how seasoned his arguments or mild his conversation. Nor did he immediately prevail with Sir John and Lady Walsh.

On one occasion, certain "beneficed doctors" held a supper with the Walshes without the presence of the disturbing Tyndale. Here they talked "at will and pleasure, uttering their blindness and ignorance without any resistance or gainsaying." Returning home, the Walshes called Tyndale and related the conversations of the evening. When Tyndale corrected the prelates' doctrine with the scriptures, Lady Walsh skeptically replied, "Well, there was such a doctor who may dispend [spend] a hundred pounds, and another two hundred pounds, and another three hundred pounds: and what! Were it reason, think you, that we should believe you before them?"[5] The association of wealth and position with knowledge and truth was not easy to surmount, but Tyndale had an idea that swung the balance in his favor.

HANDBOOK FOR A CHRISTIAN KNIGHT

Rather than reply, Tyndale bided his time and drew to his defense the most respected mind of the day, that of Erasmus. His ally was Erasmus' book the *Enchiridion Militis Christiani*. *Enchiridion* is a Greek word for "handbook"—a handbook for the *Militis Christiani*, the Christian soldier or knight. The book, whose thesis arose from Paul's counsel in Ephesians that the faithful "put on the whole armour of God" (Ephesians 6:11), was extremely popular throughout Europe. Tyndale translated it from Latin into English for his employers. The power of the *Enchiridion* lay not only in its logic and sound morals but also in its emphasis on the study of scripture and its reliance upon holy writ to validate all claims of religious truth.

Up to this point, salvation depended upon the church, and authority resided in her officers. But the word alone represented a powerful authority, and salvation rested in repentance and the atoning mercy of Christ. An alternative voice for mankind was sounding, and the richness of its tones struck responsive ears.

The Christian knight's sword was God's word sheathed in the pages of the Testaments. The word constituted a higher authority than the clergy or the bishops of Rome. Tyndale was naturally drawn to Erasmus' handbook. The common man needed the armor and sword that only God's word, plainly and openly read, could provide. Tyndale no doubt agreed, and hoped his patrons would agree, with such words as the following: "Honourest thou the bones of Paul hid in a shrine and honourest thou not the mind of Paul hid in his writings? Magnifiest thou a piece of his carcass shining through a glass and regardest not thou the whole mind of Paul shining through his letters?"[6] Tyndale's translation did the trick.

"He delivered [it] to his master and lady; who, after they had read and well perused the same, the doctorly prelates were no more so often called to the house, neither had they the cheer and countenance when they came, as before they had: which thing they marking, and well perceiving, and supposing no less but it came by the means of Master Tyndale, refrained themselves, and at last utterly withdrew, and came no more there."[7]

The Prelates' Revenge

Having been bested (though they knew not how) by an upstart youth, a mere tutor of children unworthy to share the same table with them, the prelates plotted their revenge. Beaten in the dining hall, they were determined not to be defeated in an arena they knew well, that of the church. In private they railed upon Tyndale, denouncing him as a heretic, the one accusation, if they could make it stick, that was sure to silence the voice that probed too deeply into their own failings. Tyndale found himself an accused defendant before the authorities of the diocese.

Troubling information—some true, some invented—had been given to John Bell, the bishop's chancellor. This was serious business, for heretics were burned, and the bishop's chancellor was the authority responsible to see that it was done, attending the executions in person. Bell had dealt with Lollard heretics already and knew the remedy. He was harsh and unsympathetic, a man to be wary of. Two accounts of Tyndale's first dangerous brush with the stake have survived—one recorded by Tyndale and one reported by Richard Webb to John Foxe.

"There was a sitting of the bishop's chancellor appointed, and warning was given to the priests to appear, amongst whom Master Tyndale was also warned to be there," Foxe reports. "And whether he had any misdoubt by their threatenings, or knowledge given him that they would lay some things to his charge, it is uncertain; but certain this is (as he himself declared), that he doubted their privy accusations; so that he by the way, in going thitherwards, cried in his mind heartily to God, to give him strength fast to stand in the truth of his word."[8]

The environment was openly hostile. Tyndale was accused of being "an heretic in Sophistry, an heretic in Logic, an heretic in his divinity and so continueth. But they said unto him, you bear yourself boldly of the Gentlemen here in this country, but you shall be otherwise talked with."[9] This last threatening comment referred to the protection Sir John Walsh had provided him, not to mention Sir John's wife's family. She was a Poyntz, and they held considerable power in the vicinity and beyond. A relative of Lady Walsh, Thomas Poyntz, would later selflessly render aid to Tyndale.

Tyndale wrote his account of the Little Sodbury troubles in the preface to his Pentateuch, published in 1530. Speaking of the jealous nature of his antagonists, he wrote: "When they come together to the ale house, which is their preaching-place, they affirm that my sayings are heresy. And besides that they add to of their own heads, which I never spake, as the manner is to prolong the tale to short the time withal, and accused me secretly to the chancellor and other [of] the bishop's officers."[10]

One disparity of the inquisition was that accusers were allowed to remain secret. Often the accused did not know who was informing against them, nor the specific nature of the charge. With no chance to face his adversaries, the accuser had to prove his innocence nevertheless.

"And, indeed, when I came before the chancellor," Tyndale recalled, "he threatened me grievously, and reviled me, and rated me as though I had been a dog; and laid to my charge whereof there could be none accuser brought forth, (as their manner is not to bring forth the accuser,) and yet all the priests of the country were the same day there."[11]

ALONE IN THE LION'S DEN

Alone in the lion's den, surrounded by silent smiles of satisfaction, Tyndale stood his ground with meek yet firm words. "I am content," he said, "that you bring me where you will into any country within England, giving me ten pounds a year to live with. So you bind me to nothing, but to teach children and preach."[12]

It was a disarming answer and one that invited no contentious reply. The chancellor, having spent his oratory fury and not desirous of provoking the Walsh and Poyntz families, let the matter end with the rebuke and threat. He had slim evidence of heresy and knew it, disappointing as it was to the others in the room. Yet there was gratification in the perception that the too-knowledgeable, Greek-reading Bible quoter from Oxford and Cambridge had been put in his place. Had they known what the impertinent young man would one day do, they would have made the heresy charge stick. For now he had been humbled, and that was enough.

The encounter was a turning point for Tyndale. Unless he remained silent, which he was not content to do, another attack was certain. Then, perhaps, even his powerful friends could not save him. Presently he received warning of his still-imminent danger.

"There dwelt not far off a certain doctor, that had been an old chancellor before to a bishop, who had been of old familiar acquaintance with Master Tyndale, and also favoured him well: unto whom Master Tyndale went, and opened his mind upon divers questions of the scriptures: for to him he durst be bold to disclose his heart. Unto whom the doctor said, . . . Beware what you say . . . it will cost you your life."[13]

"If God Spare My Life"

For Tyndale, the problem lay in ignorance of the word. If scripture were open for all to read, surely all would come to the same conclusion because they could discern the difference between present practices and the true teachings of Jesus and his disciples. Both the wheelwright and the priest needed a Bible they could read in the simple, strong language of the mother tongue. With his acquired and God-given skills, could Tyndale make such a translation? Reflecting on this crucial point in his life, he wrote:

"Which thing only moved me to translate the new Testament. Because I had perceived by experience, how that it was impossible to establish the lay-people in any truth, except the scripture were plainly laid before their eyes in their mother-tongue, that they might see the process, order, and meaning of the text. . . . When I was so turmoiled in the country where I was, that I could no longer there dwell, . . . I [on] this-wise thought in myself: This I suffer because the priests of the country be unlearned."[14]

Ironically, all attempts to silence him awakened a shout within, one that soon sounded from cottage and cathedral. The resolve that had lingered in the shadows of his mind since those early Oxford days now emerged into the broad open sunlight. There it stayed, growing stronger with each passing year and each effort to stop him until he uttered his final prayer with the sticks piled around him and the rope drawing tight against his throat just seconds before his death. If his own experience was not enough, had not the great Erasmus drawn the map Tyndale was now adamantly committed to follow? In the preface to his Greek New Testament, Erasmus had written these moving and inspired words:

"I vehemently dissent from those who are unwilling that the sacred scriptures, translated into the vulgar tongue, should be read by private persons. Christ wishes his mysteries to be published as widely as possible. I would wish even all women to read the gospel and the epistles of St. Paul, and I wish that they were translated into all languages of all Christian people, that they might be read and known, not merely by the Scotch and the Irish, but even by the Turks and the Saracens. I wish that the husbandman may sing parts of them at his plow, that the weaver may warble them at his shuttle, that the traveller may with their narratives beguile the weariness of the way."[15]

Tyndale took these words to heart. That his life's calling was well founded before he left Little Sodbury for London is attested to in what may have been his most famous declaration. Though he had escaped a close brush with imprisonment or fire, Tyndale was not content to sink into silent complacency or the safety of the status quo. Soon after his arraignment before the church authorities, he threw down the gauntlet.

"Master Tyndale happened to be in the company of a learned man, and in communing and disputing with him drove him to that issue, that the learned man said: 'We were better be without God's law than the pope's.' Master Tyndall, hearing that answered him: 'I defy the pope and all his laws'; and said: 'If God spare my life, ere many years *I will cause a boy that driveth the plough shall know more of the scripture than thou dost.*'"[16]

Three hundred years later, a fourteen-year-old ploughboy in Palmyra, New York, would reflect over and over on the testimony of James—a testimony put into heart-riveting English by William Tyndale.

NOTES

1. Also spelled Welch in some sources.
2. Foxe, *Acts and Monuments,* 5:117.
3. Ibid., 5:115.
4. Daniell, *William Tyndale,* 78.
5. Foxe, *Acts and Monuments,* 5:115–16.
6. Erasmus, *Enchiridion,* 115–16; spelling standardized.
7. Foxe, *Acts and Monuments,* 5:116.
8. Ibid.
9. Foxe, *Acts and Monuments* (1563), 513–14, as cited in Daniell, *William Tyndale.*
10. Greenslade, *Work of William Tindale,* 97.
11. Ibid., 97.
12. Foxe, *Acts and Monuments* (1563), 514, as cited in Daniell, *William Tyndale.*
13. Ibid., 5:116–17.
14. Greenslade, *Work of William Tindale,* 96.
15. Erasmus, in Mozley, *William Tyndale,* 34.
16. Foxe, *Acts and Monuments* (1563), 514, as cited in Daniell, *William Tyndale;* emphasis added; punctuation standardized.

"No Place in All England"

As pertaining to good deeds therefore, do the best thou canst, and desire God to give strength to do better daily; but in Christ put thy trust, and in the pardon and promises that God hath made thee for his sake; and on that rock build thine house, and there dwell. For there only shalt thou be sure from all storms and tempests, and from all wily assaults.

—WILLIAM TYNDALE, *The Obedience of a Christian Man*

"So I Gat Me to London"

What to do now occupied the center of Tyndale's reflections. The resentment of the priests increased against him to the extent that "they never ceased barking and rating at him, and laid many things sorely to his charge, saying that he was a heretic . . . ," Foxe wrote. "Being so molested and vexed . . . [he] was constrained to leave that country, and to seek another place."[1]

Tyndale realized that where to translate was not nearly as important as who would sponsor his translation. His main obstacle was a document called the Constitutions of Oxford, which he had to get around. In response to bitter opposition against Wycliffe and the Lollards, the archbishop of Canterbury, Thomas Arundel, held a convocation at Oxford in 1408 and passed numerous laws designed to eradicate the menace. The new laws forbade anyone of his own initiative to translate any portion of the scriptures into English, or to read any such translation without the approval of a bishop or council.

Violators were excommunicated, condemned as heretics, or worse. This law had doomed the seven martyrs of Coventry. Tyndale desired not only to translate into the vernacular but also to have his translation published and read by every tinker's son!

He needed the patronage of a powerful bishop, and he turned hopefully to the new bishop of London, Cuthbert Tunstall. "As I this thought," Tyndale wrote, "the bishop of London came to my remembrance, whom Erasmus . . . praiseth exceedingly . . . for his great learning. Then thought I, if I might come to this man's service, I were happy. And so I gat me to London."[2]

Tunstall was a logical choice. Sir Thomas More was Tunstall's friend and called attention to his education and character in his famous work, *Utopia*. Tunstall was a humanist scholar, a generous and liberal patron, versed in Greek, and a former student of Oxford and Cambridge. He had spent years studying in Italy and had helped Erasmus with a later edition of his Greek New Testament. He represented the openness of a new generation. Here was hope indeed, for as bishop of London, Tunstall had the necessary authority to override the Constitutions of Oxford. All indicators seemed to favor Tyndale's hope that Tunstall would support his aspirations.

Tyndale's expectations of such powerful patronage reveal a guileless innocence felt in his words: "If I might come to this man's service, I were happy." His spirit, no doubt, lifted as he traveled eastward to London, away from the petty jealousies of his own provincial clergy. One so learned as Tunstall would surely share his enthusiasm and see the logic of his proposal.

Tyndale should have realized, however, that one of the most powerful men in the country might not be excited about skirting a law whose punishment included the stake in favor of an obscure youth whose last occupation was a tutor of small boys. We are reminded of a similar innocence in Joseph Smith when he related his vision to "one of the Methodist preachers." When his testimony was treated "with great contempt," Joseph "was greatly surprised at his behavior" (Joseph Smith–History 1:21). Someone more versed

King Henry VIII, in council.

in the ways of the world might have said to Joseph, "What did you expect?" Tyndale too would be disappointed in the man to whom he now eagerly turned.

Tyndale also felt anxious for Sir John and Lady Walsh, who had been his defenders. Bringing them into his confidence, he expressed his concerns in the solicitous manner characteristic of his nature. "Sir, I perceive that I shall not be suffered to tarry long here in this country, neither shall you be able, though you would, to keep me out of the hands of the spirituality; and also what displeasure might grow thereby to you by keeping me, God knoweth; for the which I should be right sorry."[3]

But Sir John did Tyndale a final service. He sent him to a friend, Sir Harry Gilford, who had good connections in the court of Henry VIII as "Master of the Horse" and "Controller of the Royal Household." Sir Harry was a classical scholar in his own right and knew Erasmus. He would be naturally sympathetic to the novice Greek academic and could secure the coveted interview with Tunstall upon which all Tyndale's hopes rested.

With such a good introduction, William must have let his expectations soar even higher as he hurried to London. But he needed something else to persuade Tunstall. He was untested in the scholarly field, so he translated a difficult piece of Greek classical literature into English as a specimen of his talent. It appears Tyndale did not entertain the thought that the very project in question was doomed to denial, or perhaps in his zeal he merely pushed his fears to the background. His prime worry was convincing Tunstall that he was qualified for the task. The need for an English translation of the scriptures was so blatantly obvious it needed no argument to recommend it.

"So I gat me to London, and, through the acquaintance of my master, came to sir Harry Gilford, the king's grace's comproller, and brought him an Oration of Isocrates, which I had translated out of Greek into English, and desired him to speak unto my lord of London [Bishop Tunstall] for me; which he also did, as he shewed me, and willed me to write an epistle to my lord, and to go to him myself; which I also did, and delivered my epistle to a servant of his own, one William Hebilthwayte, a man of mine old acquaintance."[4]

His choice of Isocrates would show his competence in translating as well as the ability of English to carry the weight of penetrating, engaging, and substantial literature. All seemed to portend a successful conclusion, including the knowledge that a former acquaintance was serving the bishop and would present his introductory letter. But in hindsight, Tyndale should have known that he would fail in London.

"A Still Saturn"

Europe was fevered with Luther's reform. His 1522 New Testament translated into German was circulating on the Continent. The first edition sold out in ten weeks. But in London, a famous burning of all of Luther's books at St. Paul's Cross had occurred as recently as May 21, 1521, under the auspices of the celebrated Cardinal Wolsey. There, "before an enormous crowd," the cardinal sat on a chair "under a canopy of cloth of gold, attended by a brilliant throng of peers, bishops and foreign ambassadors" as the hated writings were brought forth in loads.[5]

A zealous harangue by Bishop John Fisher preceded the bonfire, and afterward all felt that the Lord's work had been done. The blackened stones of the street were testament enough that any threat to the church would be met with fierce resistance. Considering the times, why should Bishop Tunstall, despite his humanist leanings and Greek education, risk himself for an uncelebrated priest who wanted to do an end run around the Constitutions of Oxford?

There was no guarantee that Tyndale's reputation as a troublemaker and near heretic had not preceded him to London. If so, though Tunstall was not courageous enough to compromise the Constitutions of Oxford, he was at least mild in his audience with Tyndale, whose request alone could have been treated as heretical. Tyndale later described the long-anticipated interview with the bishop:

"But God (which knoweth what is within hypocrites,) saw that I was beguiled, and that that counsel was not the next way unto my purpose. And therefore he gat me no favour in my lord's sight. Whereupon my lord answered me, his house was full; he had more than he could well find; and advised me to seek in London, where he said I could not lack a service." Decidedly dejected, Tyndale realized "there was no room in my lord of London's palace to translate the new Testament."[6]

Tyndale was an unsophisticated and plain man, who in his own words was not adept in the intrigues and delicacy of the English establishment. His power lay in the pen, not in courting potentates. In a letter to his close friend, John Frith, Tyndale described himself as "evil-favoured in this world and without grace in the sight of men, speechless and rude, dull and slowwitted."[7] He was like other men called to perform God's work, including Joseph Smith, self-described as "an obscure boy . . . of no consequence in the world" (Joseph Smith–History 1:22).

Tyndale described Tunstall as "a still Saturn, that so seldom speaketh, but walketh up and down all day musing."[8] In time, that silent musing would erupt in a vigorous campaign to destroy William and disrupt the smuggling of his New Testament into England. Yet, Tyndale had an ally who was watching and directing events in his favor. As his own words indicated, he came to realize that this early disappointment proceeded from God, who was orchestrating his way and would in time bring him to a better situation to fulfill divine purposes. Had Tyndale commenced in England, his work and life would surely have been brief.

THE ENGLISH EXCEPTION

The irony of Tyndale's situation could not have escaped him. He was not asking to do something novel and unheard of. Vernacular translations of the Bible had already been rendered in German (1466), Italian (1471), French (1474), Czech (1475), Dutch (1477), Catalan (1478), and Danish (1524).[9] These were taken from the

Latin Vulgate, but they were available and for the most part without proscription. Why should there be such vehement opposition in England? In time, the Catholic Church would produce in English the Rheims New Testament, but that did not occur until 1582, and it still came from the Vulgate. The wish of Erasmus and Tyndale that "the ploughboy" have the holy word in his own tongue still grated on the authorities. Such an uncelebrated laborer, in fact, is mentioned in hauntingly familiar phraseology in the preface to the Rheims edition.

"Yet we must not imagine that in the primitive Church . . . the translated Bibles into the vulgar tongues, were in the hands of every husbandman, artificer, prentice, boy, girl, mistress, maid, man. . . . *No, in those better times men were neither so ill, nor so curious of themselves, so to abuse the blessed book of Christ. . . . The poor ploughman,* could then in labouring the ground, sing the hymns and psalms either in known or unknown languages, as they heard them in the holy Church, though they could neither read nor know the sense, meaning and mysteries of the same."[10]

The catchwords "better times," "so curious of themselves," "abuse the blessed book," and "poor ploughman" hardly veil the continued distaste a ploughman's Bible excited among the prelates and surely reflect their knowledge of Erasmus' desires and Tyndale's Little Sodbury challenge.

THE NEW "SCRIPTURE MEN"

Though rebuffed, Tyndale was not without friends. The Lord did not let his enterprise die, nor was Tyndale ready to give up. Help came in the form of one Humphrey Monmouth and the wool merchants of London. "Being refused of the bishop he came to Humphrey Mummuth, alderman of London, and besought him to help him: who the same time took him into his house, where the said Tyndale lived like a good priest, studying both night and day."[11]

Monmouth was reform-minded, as were many of his fellow merchants. He was a well-respected, prominent businessman. Wool was an economic staple in England, and even the most powerful hesitated to probe too deeply into the comings and goings of men who contributed so lucratively to the country's economic base. The dominance of the woolen industry is seen today in names like Weaver, Fuller, Sherman, Dyer, and Tucker and in phrases and words such as "dyed in the wool," "spin a yarn," "unravel a mystery," "web of life," "homespun," and "spinster."[12] The merchants were powerful friends who supported Tyndale until his death. They wanted answers more than ritual, and knowledge rather than clerical authority. Tyndale had found some kindred spirits.

Foxe calls Monmouth a "scripture-man" who "began to smell the gospel," and he tells a story about how Monmouth consistently helped a poor neighbor who later snubbed him when he discovered Monmouth's religious leanings. "The poor man, offended at what he now heard at the other's table, came no more to his house, borrowed no more money, and even accused him before the bishops." In time, Monmouth asked the poor man, "Whence is this displeasure against me?" His gentle manner brought his adversary to his knees, begging forgiveness, which was frankly offered, "and they loved one another as well as ever they did afore."[13]

"I NEVER SAW HIM WEAR LINEN"

Monmouth's friendship with Tyndale would later earn him an arraignment before Sir Thomas More. Monmouth was part of a clandestine group known as the Christian Brethren, also referred to as "known men." In time, they would subsidize Tyndale's forbidden religious publications and convey them into England from the Continent with their trading goods. From Monmouth's defense in the Tower of London, we gain valuable information about Tyndale's London period.

"They examined me . . . what exhibition [money] I did give to anybody beyond the sea. I said, None in three years past. . . . I told them, in four years past I did give unto a priest called Sir William Tyndal. . . . Upon four years and a half past and more I heard the foresaid Sir William . . . preach two or three sermons at St. Dunstan's-in-the-West in London: and after that I chanced to meet with him, and with communication I examined what living he had. He said he had none at all, but he trusted to be with my lord of London in his service: and therefore I had the better fantasy to him. And afterward he went to my lord, and spake to him, as he told me, and my lord of London answered him that he had chaplains enough, and he said to him that he would have no more at that time. And so the priest came to me again, and besought me to help him, and so I took him into my house half a year; and there he lived like a good priest, as me thought. He studied most part of the day and of the night at his book, and he would eat but sodden meat by his good will, nor drink but small single beer. I never saw him wear linen about him in the space he was with me."[14]

As in Gloucestershire, Tyndale preached while he was in London. St. Dunstan's-in-the-West was a reform-minded parish. It was not Monmouth's home parish, and he had to travel to hear Tyndale preach. What he heard obviously impressed him, for he had copies of Tyndale's sermons, which he later burned "for fear of the translator more than for any ill that I knew by them."[15] Had the sermons survived, they would have revealed Tyndale's early approach to the scriptures. We learn from Monmouth that Tyndale continued to invest long hours of study "at his book"—a probable reference to Erasmus' Greek New Testament. The reference to "sodden meat" (without spices or sauces and boiled instead of roasted), "small single beer" (weak and watered down), and the absence of "linen" in his wardrobe (wool being less expensive but unpleasant because it scratched the skin) show the modesty of Tyndale's lifestyle, a simplicity he maintained to his martyrdom.

"No Place in All England"

For half a year, Tyndale pondered his future. All avenues seemed to close as he approached them, but the fire in his bones would not abate. During his stay in London, he "marked the course of the world, and heard our praters, (I would say our preachers,) how they boasted themselves and their high authority; and beheld the pomp of our prelates, and how busy they were, as they yet are, to set peace and unity in the world, (though it be not possible for them that walk in darkness to continue long in peace) . . . and saw things whereof I defer to speak at this time, and understood at the last not only that there was no room in my lord of London's palace to translate the new Testament, but also that there was no place to do it in all England, as experience doth now openly declare."[16]

The "course of the world" was one of confusion despite all efforts to unify it. Such confusion is reminiscent of young Joseph Smith's bewilderment over the various cries of his day. "I often said to myself: What is to be done?" he humbly wondered. "Who of all these parties are right; or, are they all wrong together? If any one of them be right, which is it, and how shall I know it?" (Joseph Smith–History 1:10). Tyndale had foreseen this type of dilemma, for Joseph's anguished words echo in the conclusions the young priest drew during his last months in London. Addressing the clergy, he wrote:

"Moreover, seeing that one of you ever preacheth contrary to another; and when two of you meet, the one disputeth and brawleth with the other, as it were two scolds; and forasmuch as one holdeth this doctor, and another that . . . so that if thou hadst but of every author one book, thou couldst not pile them up in any warehouse in London, and every author is one contrary unto another. *In so great diversity of spirits, how shall I know who lieth, and who sayeth truth? Whereby shall I try and judge them? Verily by God's word, which only is true. But how shall I that do, when thou wilt not let me see scripture?"*[17]

Tyndale's acquaintance with Humphrey Monmouth brought him in contact with other merchants who had knowledge of the publishing world on the Continent. Printing was more advanced there, especially in Germany, and printers took on projects that involved risks the few printers of London would not venture.

Tyndale had tried every open, legal avenue he could and had met with opposition, threat, and hypocrisy. He would now, as had the Lollards before him, go underground. The English people would have the word of God one way or the other, even if he had to sacrifice his homeland and his life. New friends soon provided him with monetary means to live, translate, and publish in Europe.

"I did promise him £10 [pounds] sterling to pray for my father and mother their souls and all Christian souls; I did pay it him when he made his exchange to Hamborow [Hamburg]," Monmouth said. "Afterwards he got of some other men £10 sterling more, the which he left with me; and within a year after, he sent for his £10 to me from Hamborow; and thither I sent it him by one Hans Collenbeke, as I remember is his name, a merchant of the Steelyard."[18]

The London Steelyard, on the Thames, was a center for Germanic merchants living in London.[19] Searching for contraband publications, Sir Thomas More would later raid the area. Meanwhile, with at least ten pounds in his purse, his Greek New Testament in his baggage, and safe contacts in Germany, Tyndale left England for Hamburg. He never saw his native land again.

As Tyndale biographer J. F. Mozley concludes, "He was content to be without his country, that he might serve his country. He goes not for his own sake, but to safeguard the great work committed to his trust."[20]

Notes

1. Foxe, *Acts and Monuments,* 5:117.
2. Greenslade, *Work of William Tindale,* 97.
3. Foxe, *Acts and Monuments,* 5:117.
4. Greenslade, *Work of William Tindale,* 97.
5. Dickens, *The English Reformation,* 91.
6. Greenslade, *Work of William Tindale,* 97–98.
7. Ibid., 114.
8. Tyndale, *Practice of Prelates,* 337.
9. Daniell, *William Tyndale,* 93.

10. Rheims, *The New Testament of Jesus Christ,* sig. a, iii, in Daniell, *William Tyndale,* 95; emphasis added.

11. Foxe, *Book of Martyrs,* 179.

12. Bobrick, *Wide As the Waters,* 97.

13. Mozley, *William Tyndale,* 44–45.

14. Ibid., 46.

15. Ibid., 49.

16. Greenslade, *Work of William Tindale,* 97–98.

17. Ibid., 90; emphasis added.

18. Mozley, *William Tyndale,* 46.

19. The "Steelyard," which probably comes from the Low German word *stâl-gard,* meaning courtyard, was established by an organization of German merchant communities located in London called the Hanseatic League.

20. Mozley, *William Tyndale,* 49–50.

FLIGHT AND
FLIGHT AGAIN

𝔥e is our Redeemer, Deliverer, Reconciler, Mediator,
Intercessor, Advocate, Attorney, Solicitor, our Hope, Comfort,
Shield, Protection, Defender, Strength, Health, Satisfaction
and Salvation. His blood, his death, all that he ever did, is ours.
And Christ himself, with all that he is or can do, is ours. . . .
And God (as great as he is) is mine, with all that he hath,
through Christ and his purchasing.

—WILLIAM TYNDALE, *A PATHWAY INTO THE HOLY SCRIPTURE*

"INFLAMED WITH A TENDER CARE"

In proclaiming Tyndale's departure from England, Foxe
observed that he was motivated by his love for the simple
word of God and for the English poor of his country.
"Therefore, having by God's providence some aid ministered unto
him by Humphrey Mummuth, and certain other good men, he . . .
departed into Germany, where the good man, being inflamed with a
tender care and zeal of his country, refused no travail nor diligence,
how, by all means possible, to reduce his brethren and countrymen
of England to the same taste and understanding of God's holy Word
and verity . . . that the poor people might read and see the simple
plain Word of God," Foxe wrote.[1]

When Tyndale reached Germany, the country was in the throes
of the Lutheran Reformation. Fierce debates, centered on the
Augustinian monk who dared challenge the authority of a 1,500-
year-old church, raged. A whole new order was beginning. The age

of controlling religious authority was being replaced with reason, conscience, and individual choice, and, after the fury of religious war was spent, tolerance. In Germany some cities were safe for a would-be translator; others were still uncompromisingly dangerous.

Tyndale's first stop was Hamburg, as Humphrey Monmouth's testimony verifies, but all contemporary evidence suggests that he soon went to Wittenberg—bastion of the formidable Luther, who had just finished his "September Testament" in German in 1522. One German prince called Wittenberg "the common asylum of all apostates."[2] It was a logical destination. Hamburg was a great trading center and a sound choice for smuggling Bibles into England, but it was still a papal city. Wittenberg, by contrast, had a university, books, and scholars with which to confer. Luther's reforming companion, Philipp Melanchthon, was a professor of Greek, and Hebrew, a novelty, was also studied in Wittenberg. The environment, for one of the few times in Tyndale's life, was safe. Here he could work without fear.

AN EARLY ALIAS

Sir Thomas More and John Foxe both verify that Tyndale visited Luther in Wittenberg. No official record survives of such a visit, but Luther and Tyndale were present in the city at the same time, and it would be surprising if Tyndale did not seek a conference with the leading reformer of the day. Many of Luther's ideas found their way into Tyndale's earliest writings, including the prologue to his first published manuscript of Matthew. Association with Luther would explain much of the violent opposition Tyndale later experienced, as would his advocacy of salvation by faith in Christ alone—a Lutheran doctrine—rather than by the sacraments of the Catholic Church.

Mozley discovered William's name in the registers of Wittenberg University but disguised as *Guillelmus* (William) *Daltici ex Anglia.* Reversing the syllables of Tindal yields "Daltin," which is close to *Daltici.* This name was listed in the registers with Matthias von Emerson, nephew to Margaret von Emerson of Hamburg, who later sheltered Tyndale and with whom he probably stayed when he first left England. These were dangerous times, and Tyndale had already begun to form his secretive ways. A later English martyr named Robert Barnes attended Wittenberg using the alias *Antonius Anglus*—his real name added in the margin by Melanchthon.[3]

Tyndale must have known he could find friendship with the von Emerson family in Hamburg through the German merchants of the London Steelyard. Perhaps Margaret convinced him to travel with her nephew to Wittenberg, where he finished his first translation of the New Testament in about nine months and mastered German. Returning to Hamburg, he lodged with the von Emerson family again while waiting for money from England to finance printing.

WILLIAM ROYE

While at Wittenberg, Tyndale teamed up with William Roye, a lapsed English friar from Greenwich considered an apostate by the Catholic Church. His name was also listed with Tyndale in the registers of Wittenberg. Though he had failings and was not Tyndale's first choice, Roye became his first helper in the printing process nonetheless.

"While I abode [waited for] a faithful companion, which now hath taken another voyage upon him, to preach Christ where, I supposed, he was never yet preached, (God, which put in his heart thither to go, send his Spirit with him, comfort him, and bring his purpose to good effect!) one William Roye, a man somewhat crafty, when he cometh unto new acquaintance, and before he be thorough known, and namely when all is spent, came unto me and offered his help. As long as he had no money, somewhat I could rule him; but as soon as he had gotten him money, he became like himself again. Nevertheless, I suffered all things till that was ended, which I could not do alone without one, both to write, and to help me to compare the texts together. When that was ended, I took my leave, and bade him farewell for our two lives, and (as men say) a day longer."[4]

The identity of the "faithful companion" Tyndale favored as

scribe remains a mystery. Later, Miles Coverdale came to Antwerp to help him with the books of Moses. Perhaps it was he. Foxe indicates that Tyndale, "considering in his mind, and conferring also with John Frith," decided the scriptures must go to the common people.[5] Could Frith have been the longed-for companion? He was like a son to Tyndale, as evidenced in private letters written just before Frith's burning.

If Tyndale had a weakness, it was his trusting nature. He too easily believed that men would be true and unselfish, and that they would share the same noble vision he held. Assuming the best in his fellowmen often led to sad consequences. Such a noble trait should not be labeled weakness, even though betrayal by one whom Tyndale called "friend" eventually led to his death. In this he was not unlike Joseph Smith, whose personality attracted the deeply loyal as well as the devious and weak, such as John C. Bennett and William Law. Though helpful, William Roye jeopardized all Tyndale worked for, and as soon as possible Tyndale parted company with him. For the time being, his labor was too critical for him not to make use of Roye.

"HEATED WITH WINE"

His translation of the New Testament finished, Tyndale now pondered where to have it printed. He needed a city close to his merchant connections and with access to shipping. He had three likely choices—Hamburg, Cologne, and Antwerp. Cologne and Antwerp had excellent printing houses and strong connections to English merchants. Antwerp was the main trading center of Europe and in time became Tyndale's base, but for unknown reasons he decided on Cologne. Cologne, though somewhat neutral toward reform, had a strong Catholic fervor and was not safe, but it was on the Rhine with easy access to shipping bound for England. Tyndale arrived in the summer of 1525 with Roye and his completed manuscript and agreed with the printing house of Peter Quentell to produce the first printed English New Testament.

Things went well at first. Tyndale no doubt rejoiced in the fruits of his dream. The smell of ink, the noise of the press, and the sight of newly printed pages with the words "When Jesus was born at Bethlehem" must have produced strong emotions. But secrecy was demanded, for Tyndale's initiative was a dangerous one. Sadly, William Roye was not a man to keep silent. Tyndale described him as one "whose tongue is able not only to make fools stark mad, but also to deceive the wisest, that is, at the first sight and acquaintance."[6] He spoke from personal experience.

An unknown enemy named John Dobneck walked the streets of Cologne. Known by his Latin name *Cochlaeus* (snail), he was a bitter opponent of the reforming spirit. When Luther's German New Testament began to be read by the likes of tailors, shoemakers, and women, Dobneck was incensed. That many were memorizing whole sections and then debating openly with the clergy distressed him. The world would end in chaos if these alarming events were not checked. Reformers had driven Dobneck from his post as dean of St. Mary's in Frankfurt and then from Mainz, in west Germany. He had personal grudges to settle with those who dared compromise the Catholic faith. He was so proud of stopping Tyndale in Cologne that he wrote three separate accounts of it, including the following:

"Two English apostates hoped . . . that they might through the printing-press multiply by many thousands the testament thus translated, and convey it thence secretly under cover of other merchandise to England. Such was their confidence of success, that at the first onset they asked the printers for an edition of six thousand [a considerable run for the times]. The printers, however, fearing that if any mishap occurred, they would suffer very heavy loss, put only three thousand to press; and if these were happily sold, they could easily print afresh."[7]

Tyndale's request for a run of six thousand shows his confidence in the English market. He was sure his New Testament would sell, even at the risk of the buyer's life. John Dobneck recalled that the reformers were "so puffed up with vain confidence, that in their uncontrollable joy they made known the secret before its time."[8] He

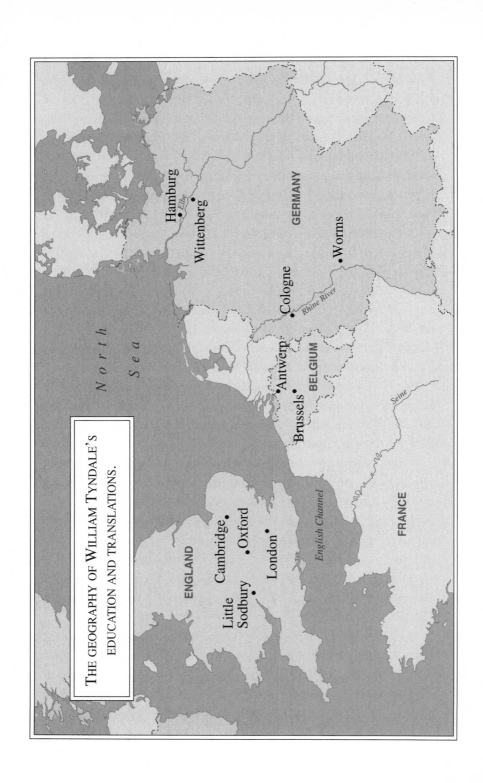

THE GEOGRAPHY OF WILLIAM TYNDALE'S
EDUCATION AND TRANSLATIONS.

was not talking about Tyndale, whose nature was not given to boasting, but about Roye. The printers were not halfway through the Gospels, but Roye's foolish tongue had triumphed prematurely in their ears, revealing their plans, their financial backing from merchant friends, and the talent behind it all.

Unfortunately, Dobneck was also printing religious books with Peter Quentell. While on a visit, he heard the printers talk about the English New Testament. Feigning friendship, he invited them to his lodging, "and when they were heated with wine, one of them in more private talk revealed to him the secret."[9] Despite Henry VIII or Cardinal Wolsey, the tipsy printers revealed, all of England would soon be Lutheran. The Englishmen responsible for the translation were skilled in languages and had the backing of merchants who planned to smuggle the books into English ports. Before anyone was aware of the clandestine importation, the whole of England would have the New Testament in English. The full scheme came tumbling out in a wine-induced revelation before the astonished Dobneck.

THE FOX ESCAPES THE TRAP

Dobneck mulled over the information and then secretly revealed what he had learned to Hermann Rinck, a Cologne city leader. Before acting, Rinck quietly investigated Quentell's shop to verify the report. Acting quickly, lest the fox escape the trap, Rinck and Dobneck went to the city authorities, obtained an interdiction on the work, and prepared to arrest Tyndale and Roye and destroy the translation. But an unknown friend tipped them off just in time, and the two, grabbing what printed pages they could, fled up the Rhine to Worms, a city in full support of Luther. Nevertheless, the cat was out of the bag. Dobneck and Rinck, a friend of Henry VIII, immediately wrote letters to the king, Cardinal Wolsey, and Bishop Fisher, warning them to keep a sharp eye on English ports for the dangerous contraband that would soon arrive.

Only one copy of what is called the Cologne Fragment has survived. It was found in 1834 bound with another reformer's works.

Now in the British Library, it contains a woodcut of Matthew dipping a pen into an inkpot held by an angel, Tyndale's translation up to Matthew 22:12, and a list of New Testament books in the order of Luther's September Bible (Luther listed Hebrews, James, Jude, and Revelation separately, not considering them of equal weight to the rest of the New Testament). It also includes a prologue, which gives a first glimpse of Tyndale in writing.

"FOR YOUR SPIRITUAL EDIFYING"

The mild, sweet warmth of Tyndale's initial thoughts are worthy of the book he was endeavoring to make known to his countrymen:

"I have here translated, brethren and sisters most dear and tenderly beloved in Christ, the New Testament for your spiritual edifying, consolation and solace, exhorting instantly and beseeching those that are better seen in the tongues than I, and that have higher gifts of grace to interpret the sense of the scripture and meaning of the spirit than I, to consider and ponder my labour, and that with the spirit of meekness. And if they perceive in any places that I have not attained the very sense of the tongue or meaning of the scripture, or have not given the right English word, that they put to their hands to amend it, remembering that so is their duty to do: for we have not received the gifts of God for ourselves only, or for to hide them, but for to bestow them unto the honouring of God and Christ, and edifying of the congregation, which is the body of Christ."[10]

Tyndale's words echo the sentiments Moroni shared while translating the book of Ether. His words have the same humility, the same hope that God's comforting truth would reach receptive hearts, the same fear that critics would read his efforts harshly and reject what he had diligently labored to get right, the same fear that his exertions had failed to match the dignity of the original.

"Lord, the Gentiles will mock at these things, because of our weakness in writing. . . . Thou hast also made our words powerful and great, even that we cannot write them; wherefore, when we write we behold our weakness, and stumble because of the placing of our words; and I fear lest the Gentiles shall mock at our words," Moroni said. In reply, the Lord promised to "make weak things become strong" (Ether 12:23, 25, 27). The Lord did the same for Tyndale, whose first attempts to raise the Savior's voice to the English ear ring with spirit and power.

"Blessed are the poor in spirit: *for* theirs is the kingdom of heaven," Tyndale translated in the Cologne Fragment. Notice how the eight syllables in the first phrase of the Beatitudes match the eight syllables in the second phrase, with the word *for* acting as a fulcrum that divides the sentence. The pattern follows in the second phrase, with six syllables appearing on either side of *for:* "Blessed are they that mourn: *for* they shall be comforted." Similar patterns appear in the Cologne Fragment and in the King James Version used today by The Church of Jesus Christ of Latter-day Saints, including "The last shall be first, and the first shall be last" and "For many are called, and few be chosen."

The language is plain, concise, stately, and the combinations of words are just right. David Daniell, commenting on Tyndale's fluid prose, wrote: "In his Bible translations, Tyndale's conscious use of everyday words . . . and his wonderful ear for rhythmic patterns, gave to English not only a Bible language, but a new prose. England was blessed as a nation in that the language of its principal book, as the Bible in English rapidly became, was the fountain from which flowed the lucidity, suppleness and expressive range of the greatest prose thereafter. These are qualities . . . which should ideally be read aloud."[11]

"WHO IS SO BLIND?"

Anticipating opposition, although not the hatred evident in the loud shouts of condemnation, the burning of his Testament, and his own martyrdom, Tyndale defended his actions in the prologue to Matthew. To the last, his amiable naivete and innocence remained largely unchanged.

"The causes that moved me to translate I thought better that other should imagine than that I should rehearse them. Moreover I supposed it superfluous: for *who is so blind to ask why light should be showed to them that walk in darkness, where they cannot but stumble,* and where to stumble is the danger of eternal damnation, or so despiteful that he would envy any man . . . so necessary a thing, or so bedlam mad to affirm that good is the natural cause of evil, and darkness to proceed out of light, and that lying should be grounded in truth and verity; and not rather clean contrary, that light destroyeth darkness, and verity reproveth all manner lying."[12]

Nephi, quoting Isaiah, indicated that the Book of Mormon would cause the "eyes of the blind [to] see out of obscurity and out of darkness." Describing the Gentiles in the latter days, Nephi also wrote, "Because of the many plain and precious things which have been taken out of the . . . gospel of the Lamb, an exceedingly great many do stumble." The Book of Mormon *and* the Bible, despite the "many plain and precious things taken away from the book," were sent to clarify and enlighten (2 Nephi 27:29; 1 Nephi 13:29, 28). The emergence of both in the last days is part of God's marvelous plan.

Tyndale's prologue introduces a style so familiar that we might not consider its wonder. The majority of his argument is taken directly from scripture. Hints of Isaiah, Paul's epistle to the Corinthians, and Jesus' conversation with Nicodemus are easily seen. Tyndale went straight to the word for his doctrine, not to the scholars or church fathers. That approach was entirely new for his day, though it would seem only natural for our day.

Considering his "outlaw" life and the demands of his work, Tyndale felt he could not ask a wife to live in danger and uncertainty. "If I live chaste [unmarried]," he wrote, "I do it not . . . that I look for an higher room in heaven than they shall have which live in wedlock . . . but truly to wait on the evangelion [his gospel work of translation], and to serve my brother withal."[13]

The "Philistines" Have Arrived

While Tyndale and Roye hurried up the Rhine to the safety of Worms, word raced across the channel to the king and his counselors. Henry was not yet engaged in his bitter travail with the pope over his divorce and saw himself, as his newly granted title suggested, as the Defender of the Faith. On December 2, 1525, news of Tyndale's activities came to the attention of Edward Lee, the king's almoner (one who distributed alms) and the ambassador to Spain. He quickly wrote a warning to England.

"I am certainly informed . . . that an Englishman, your subject . . . hath translated the New Testament into English, and within a few days intendeth to arrive with the same imprinted in England," Lee wrote. "I need not to advertise your grace what infection and danger may ensue hereby, if it be not withstanded. This is the next way to fulfil your kingdom with Lutherans. For all Luther's perverse opinions be grounded upon bare words of scripture. . . . All our forefathers, governors of the church of England, hath with all diligence forbad and eschewed publication of English bibles. . . . Now sir, as God hath endued your grace with Christian courage, to set forth the standard against these Philistines, and to vanquish them, so I doubt not but that he will assist your grace to prosecute and perform the same, that is to undertread them, that they shall not now again lift up their heads, which they endeavour now by means of English bibles. . . . Wherefore, lest any danger might ensue if these books secretly should be brought in, I thought my duty to advertise your grace thereof, considering that it toucheth your high honour, and the wealth and integrity of the Christian faith within your realm; which cannot long endure, if these books may come in."[14]

Perhaps without fully recognizing it, Tyndale had thrown down the gauntlet not only to the whole church structure but also to Henry VIII. Fortunately, he had learned a valuable skill in Cologne—how to disappear. For a decade, he eluded diligent and unrelenting searches by slipping in and out of cities, ports, and printing shops—doing so in a day when cities numbered well below a hundred thousand. His few surviving letters have no address or identifying marks to indicate his whereabouts. His language skills were certainly an asset, but he was a foreigner nonetheless and with limited funds. He found help from the few friends he could trust and, of course, from an overseeing God who knew the value of the words flowing from his pen.

Notes

1. Foxe, *Book of Martyrs,* 179.
2. Mozley, *William Tyndale,* 52.
3. Ibid., 53.
4. Greenslade, *Work of William Tindale,* 99.
5. Foxe, *Book of Martyrs,* 179.
6. Greenslade, *Work of William Tindale,* 100.
7. In Mozley, *William Tyndale,* 58.
8. Ibid., 58.
9. Ibid., 59.
10. Tyndale, "Cologne Prologue," in Mozley, *William Tyndale,* 62–63. The prologue was expanded and published in 1531 as *A Pathway into the Holy Scripture.*
11. Daniell, *William Tyndale,* 116.
12. Tyndale, "Cologne Prologue," in Mozley, *William Tyndale,* 62–63.
13. Mozley, *William Tyndale,* 63.
14. Ibid., 65–66.

WORMS, GERMANY

"100,000 PIECES
OF MONEY"

𝕿𝖍𝖊 scripture is the light and life of God's elect, and that mighty power wherewith God createth them, and shapeth them, after the similitude, likeness, and very fashion of Christ; and therefore sustenance, comfort, and strength to courage them, that they may stand fast, and endure, and merrily bear their soul's health, wherewith the lusts of the flesh are subdued and killed, and the spirit mollified and made soft, to receive the print of the image of our Saviour Jesus.

—WILLIAM TYNDALE, *AN EXPOSITION UPON THE FIRST EPISTLE OF JOHN*

SMUGGLING SIZE

In 1521, Martin Luther made his stand at the Diet of Worms, defying Pope Leo X and Roman emperor Charles V. It was a history-changing moment that opened the door to other reformers, including Tyndale, who fled to Worms with what he and Roye could salvage of their Cologne efforts. Worms was smaller than Cologne but much safer and firmly in the control of the reformers. Tyndale and Roye soon employed the services of Peter Schoeffer, who began printing a smaller-sized New Testament. Because of the difference in page size—Schoeffer printed Tyndale's New Testament in octavo (eight pages of text per printing sheet), while Peter Quentell printed Matthew in quarto (four pages of text per printing sheet)—the whole project was started over.

To waste the Cologne Gospel of Matthew was unthinkable. So

both the Cologne Fragment and the full Worms edition of the New Testament were shipped to England, which caused considerable confusion among those trying to keep them out. Where were all these New Testaments coming from? Paper costs constituted the major expense in printing. At the time, paper was made from old rags bought by full-time gatherers. The smaller volume cut costs considerably, making the New Testament even more affordable.

Tyndale also gave consideration to the convenience of hiding the smaller volume. Opposition was making him wiser. He was an intensely hunted man, engaged in an extremely dangerous occupation that required a certain street savvy for seller and buyer. A single misstep could cost him his life. His Worms edition was a perfect smuggling size. The first paperback-sized book to be printed, it could be hidden in the lining or tucked neatly in a sleeve of a coat or dress in, to borrow a phrase from Tyndale's 1526 New Testament, "the twinkling of an eye."

The work apparently went smoothly, and the first Greek-to-English New Testament in a portable format entered the world early in 1526, never to slip into darkness again. As Nephi had foreseen, the Gentiles would have their book—at least half of it, for the Old Testament still waited. But Nephi saw that the book "carried forth among them" contained records like those "upon the plates of brass," as well as "the fulness of the gospel of the Lord, of whom the twelve apostles bear record" (1 Nephi 13:20, 23–24). Worms had a sizeable Jewish population and provided an excellent opportunity for mastering Hebrew. England had expelled its Jews earlier, so the Lord in his wisdom brought Tyndale to the Continent, and not just for reasons of safety.

Tyndale's New Testament marked a great historical milestone in paving the way for the Restoration. The compelling words that urged a searching youth into a grove of trees—"If any that is among you lack wisdom, let him ask of God" (James 1:5)—were now boldly laid before the eyes of every ploughboy searching for truth. In his 1534 edition, Tyndale improved his translation, dropping "that is among" for the more simple "of," rendering James's promise exactly as Joseph Smith read it.

Doing Good in Secret

If Tyndale's original intention had been possible, we would not know who translated this first groundbreaking work. He did not attach his name to the translation—doing so for the purest of reasons, not fear of prosecution. For years it was thought that only two copies of the original 1526 edition had survived, both without a title page, but in 1996 a third copy surfaced in Germany, complete with a title page. As Tyndale had indicated, his name was not on it. In his preface to *The Parable of the Wicked Mammon,* he revealed why he deliberately excluded his authorship.

"The cause why I set my name before this little treatise, and have not rather done it in the New Testament, is, that then I followed the counsel of Christ, which exhorteth men (Matt. vi) to do their good deeds secretly, and to be content with the conscience of well-doing, and that God seeth us; and patiently to abide the reward of the last day, which Christ hath purchased for us: and now would I fain have done likewise, but am compelled otherwise to do."[1]

He was "compelled" to indicate his authorship because of his association with William Roye. After Roye departed from Tyndale, he joined a renegade friar named Jerome, also from Greenwich. They settled in Strasbourg and promptly proceeded to publish defamatory and distasteful rhymes sharply attacking Cardinal Wolsey. Tyndale warned Jerome about Roye's character, but his warning went unheeded. The rhymes came off the press without an author's name attached, and word had it that Tyndale was responsible. Fearing that association with such railings would compromise his precious New Testament, Tyndale detached himself totally from Roye, explaining what he had and had not published.

His dream was not yet fulfilled. The Old Testament had to be translated from the Hebrew, and the New Testament needed continual refining, so Tyndale could not afford a loss of dignity for the most critical of all publications, the Bible itself, because of cheap shots taken at the cardinal. His modesty and purity of motive are evidenced in the epilogue of the 1526 New Testament:

"Them that are learned christianly I beseech, forasmuch as I am sure, and my conscience beareth me record, that of a pure intent, singly and faithfully, *I have interpreted it, as far forth as God gave me the gift of knowledge and understanding,* that the rudeness of the work now at the first time offend them not; but that they consider how that I had no man to counterfeit [imitate—he had no previous English version to follow], neither was helped with English of any that had interpreted the same or such like thing in the scripture beforetime. *Moreover, even very necessity, and cumbrance (God is record) above strength, which I will not rehearse, lest we should seem to boast ourselves, caused that many things are lacking which necessarily are required.* Count it as a thing not having his full shape, but as it were borne before his time, even as a thing begun rather than finished."[2]

"NECESSITY, AND CUMBRANCE ABOVE STRENGTH"

Because of Tyndale's unwillingness to play the martyr's role or to boast, he largely concealed the burdens that of "necessity, and cumbrance above strength" he faced—a paraphrase of Paul's words to new converts. "We would not, brethren, have you ignorant of our trouble which came to us in Asia, that we were pressed out of measure, *above strength,* insomuch that we despaired even of life: But we had the sentence of death in ourselves, that we should not trust in ourselves, but in God which raiseth the dead" (2 Corinthians 1:8–9; emphasis added). The context of Paul's words suggests Tyndale's own trials were serious and life threatening.

Tyndale worked with German printers who were unfamiliar with English. So to ensure that the typesetter, who would not know what he was composing, transposed the manuscript correctly, Tyndale had to employ constant vigilance and scrutiny.[3] He frequented the printing shop, proofreading, making corrections, and thus placing himself in a public setting. Printers were known for hard drinking, as the Cologne troubles verified. Having survived a close call there, Tyndale would have been eager to see the final translation bound and ready for transport into England before the next onslaught by his enemies.

During the imperial diet in the summer of 1526 in Speyer, Germany, a friend to Luther named Spalatin wrote an entry in his diary that has survived to this day. At a dinner held August 11, one of the guests, Hermann von dem Busche, related that he had been to Worms and met Tyndale. Spalatin's entry reads:

"Buschius told us that at Worms *six thousand copies* of the New Testament have been printed in English. The work has been translated by an Englishman, staying there with two other Britons, who is so skilled in seven tongues . . . that whichever he speaks, you would think it his native tongue. *For the English, despite the opposition and unwillingness of the king, [have been] so long after the gospel, that they affirm that they will buy the New Testament, even if they must pay 100,000 pieces of money for it."*[4]

All religious motives aside, it is easy to see why Tyndale found such support among members of the merchant class, who were willing to risk their lives and fortunes on a Bible that England was hungering to receive. The demand was ready if they could meet the supply. Obviously the hesitation Tyndale had met from the Cologne printer had been overcome, and large runs were now the standard.

THE OFFENDING WORDS

The few surviving copies of the Worms edition bear testimony to the fierce opposition it met in England. Such hostility may have resulted from Tyndale's translation of several key words the church perceived as an attack upon its most-favored traditions. Tyndale properly translated the Greek word *metanoeo* into the English word *repent,* instead of "do penance." Repent suggested a turning of the mind, an inward self-evaluation between a man and his God. Do penance, on the other hand, supported acts required by the clergy, including pilgrimage, indulgences, purgatory, and so forth. These acts provided sources of financial stability, and Tyndale was undercutting them.

He translated the Greek *ekklesia* into the English *congregation* rather than into *church*. The true body of Christ was an assembly of believers, not a professional, hierarchal organization. *Priest* became *elder* (*senior* in 1526 and improved to *elder* in 1534), and *confession of sins* became a much more simple *acknowledgment* or *admission* of them. Such a rendering would strip the formal confessional of its aura and once again threaten lucrative foundations. Essentially, Tyndale was simplifying the doctrine, making it a much more personal, individual experience based on faith in the atoning mercy of Christ, not on the sacramental rites of a concrete body.

The very nature of putting a Bible in the hands of a ploughboy took attention away from the priest performing the necessary rites to which that ploughboy looked for salvation. The *word* became dominant. Preaching the sacred narrative provided the key to Christ's saving grace as faith was created in the soul, not in the pew or at the altar.

This difference is easily seen in one of the main distinctions between Protestant and Catholic churches. In Catholic cathedrals, the altar sits in the center, the focus of worship, with the pulpit on the side, implying the supremacy of ritual and ceremony. In Protestant churches, the pulpit commands the central position, suggesting that preaching the scriptures is paramount. A Latter-day Saint chapel follows Protestant tradition, with the pulpit in the center and the sacrament table on the side. But this is not to say that teaching is more important than ordinances. In the temple, the altar occupies the focal point, from which teaching emanates. Thus, Latter-day Saint worship balances necessary ordinances with saving knowledge.

ELOQUENCE THAT SPEAKS OF HOLINESS

Even with Tyndale's challenge to some critical doctrines, it is hard to understand the fierce hatred his translation inspired. But in

The Gospell off Sancte Jhon.

The fyrst Chapter.

IN the begynnynge was that worde/ād that worde was with god: and god was thatt worde. The same was in the begynnynge wyth god. All thyngſ were made by it/ and with out it/ was made noo thige/ that made was. In it was lyfe/ And lyfe was the light of mē/ And the light ſhyneth i darcknes/ ād darcknes cōpreheded it not.

There was a mā ſent from god/ whoſe name was Jhon. The ſame cā as a witnes/ to beare witnes of thelight/ that all men through hī myght beleve. He was nott that light: but to beare witnes of the light. That was a true light/ whīch lighteneth all men that come ito the worlde. He was in the worlde/ ād the worlde by hī was made: and the worlde knewe hym not.

He cā ito his awne/ ād his receaved hī not. vnto as meny as receaved hī/ gave he power to bē the ſōnes of god: i that they beleved ō his name: which were borne not of bloude nor of the will of the fleſſhe/ nor yet of the will of men: but of god. And that worde was made fleſſhe/ and dwelt amonge vs/ and we ſawe the glory offyr/ as the glory off the only begotten ſonne off the father/

A page from a Tyndale New Testament.

the end, he won, with 90 percent of his New Testament translation finding a permanent home in the King James Bible. A few examples of his inspired rendering of the prophetic voice should be enough to convince even the most ardent skeptic of his calling. The examples below show how strongly Tyndale framed the language of faith and how easily the cadence and common, unadorned speech combine to produce a unique eloquence. If the medium does not match the holiness of the message, the sacred truth is compromised. Beauty of expression helps us live a holier life, instilling faith and courage much like music.

> For unto you is born this day in the city of David a Saviour, which is Christ the Lord. (Luke 2:11)
> Looking unto Jesus, the author and finisher of our faith. (Hebrews 12:2)
> Fight the good fight of faith. (1 Timothy 6:12)
> For in him we live, and move, and have our being. (Acts 17:28)
> Fear not, little flock. (Luke 12:32; D&C 6:34)
> For where your treasure is, there will your heart be also. (Luke 12:34)
> Ye are the light of the world. A city that is set on a hill cannot be hid. (Matthew 5:14)
> Our Father which art in heaven, Hallowed be thy name. . . . Give us this day our daily bread. . . . Lead us not into temptation, but deliver us from evil. (Matthew 6:9, 11, 13)

How did the cobbler and blacksmith feel as they read these words for the first time in beautiful English prose? The phrases are so common we may not realize the genius behind them, even in the smallest of details. Notice how the smooth flow of words jolts to an end if we drop only one syllable of Tyndale's rendering: "Knock and it shall be opened *to* you" rather than "Knock and it shall be opened *unto* you." *Unto* keeps the rhythm harmonious.

The Gift of the Word *Atonement*

One final contribution of the 1526 edition is worthy of our deepest gratitude: "We also joy in God by the means of our Lord Jesus Christ, by whom we have received this *atonement*" (Romans 5:11; emphasis added).

This verse is uniquely prized. It is the only place in the New Testament that the word *atonement* appears, yet it is the most significant word Tyndale provided for our faith. He was the first to use it in describing Christ's redeeming act. Sir Thomas More, Tyndale's enemy, used the word in a secular sense in his *History of King Richard III* in 1513, but *atonement* as it applied to Jesus made its debut in 1526. Today it is rarely used in any other context than that of the Savior's redeeming act. *Atonement* is the single word of Anglo-Saxon origin that describes a theological doctrine;[5] other doctrinal words come from Latin, Hebrew, or Greek. *Atonement* holds a prominent place in the Book of Mormon and the Doctrine and Covenants, but it is Tyndale's creation.

The Alternatives

To appreciate what this first edition of the New Testament did for the English language, we need only read translations from the Lollard manuscripts, which predate Tyndale. Lollard scriptures were essentially Latinized English. Tyndale's translation, by contrast, put the old tongues into living English. The differences are easy to hear.

Compare "Rest thou, eat, drink and make feast" with Tyndale's "Take thine ease, eat, drink, and be merry" (Luke 12:19). The repeated long "e" sound gives the phrase its distinctive quality. Compare "Not serving with the eye as pleasing to men" with Tyndale's "Not with eyeservice, as menpleasers" (Colossians 3:22).[6] Tyndale excelled at creating new words by combining two words.

Comparing Tyndale's work with modern efforts shows similar disparity. The difference is best noted when reading aloud, as illustrated by Matthew 14:28–33, in which Christ saves Peter when he walks on water. The Phillips Modern English version renders the verses as follows:

"'Lord, if it is really you,' said Peter, 'tell me to come to you on the water.' 'Come on, then,' replied Jesus. Peter stepped down from the boat and began to walk on the water, making for Jesus. But when he saw the fury of the wind he panicked and began to sink, calling out, 'Lord save me!' At once Jesus reached out his hand and caught him, saying, 'You little-faith! What made you lose your nerve like that?' Then, when they were both aboard the boat, the wind dropped. The whole crew came and knelt down before Jesus, crying, 'You are indeed the Son of God!'"

Now we turn to Tyndale:

"Peter answered and said: If thou be he, bid me come unto thee on the water. And he said, Come. And when Peter was come down out of the ship, he walked on the water to go to Jesus. But when he saw a mighty wind, he was afraid. And as he began to sink, he cried saying: Master save me. And immediately Jesus stretched forth his hand, and caught him, and said to him: O thou of little faith: wherefore didst thou doubt? And as soon as they were come into the ship, the wind ceased. Then they that were in the ship came and worshiped him, saying: Of a truth thou art the Son of God."

Tyndale set a rhythmic standard that King James translators had sense enough to follow. As they produced their Bible, they maintained the musical bar he had raised.

The Genius of Joseph Smith

Masterful examples of the gift of interpretation of tongues make Joseph Smith's translations remarkable by comparison with Tyndale's work. A testimony of the Book of Mormon and the Pearl of Great Price is enhanced by realizing that they contain the same wonderful emphasis, rhythm, proverbial wisdom in strong memorable lines, and simplicity of expression found in Tyndale's Bible translation. It is as if both men had been apprenticed to the same Master and moved by the same inspiration, which, of course, they had been. We should not be surprised. Joseph was raised in a Biblical rhetorical tradition that put him in tune with the pulse of the King James Bible. Having the gift of translation and an innate ability with language, Joseph drew on his predecessor's talents as he produced an exceptional style of his own. Those who criticize the literary value of the Book of Mormon and Pearl of Great Price simply do not know what good writing is!

When Joseph Smith needed the right English expression to give voice to Nephi's anguished cry, he echoed the words of Paul as rendered by Tyndale: "O wretched man that I am!" (2 Nephi 4:17; Romans 7:24). Though Joseph translated the Book of Mormon by the gift and power of God, he no doubt drew upon his knowledge of, and experience with, the Tyndale-inspired Bible as he produced, for example, the Savior's Sermon on the Mount in Third Nephi. The best translators seek help from every source they can. But Joseph was a master in his own right. Listen to the Tyndale-like power found in 2 Nephi 2:25: "Adam fell that men might be; and men are, that they might have joy." Notice the seven syllables before and after the word *and*. Here are other phrases familiar to every reader of the Book of Mormon:

> Look to God and live. (Alma 37:47)
> Come unto Christ. (Omni 1:26)
> The plain and most precious parts of the gospel. (1 Nephi 13:32)
> The most lost of all mankind. (Alma 24:11)
> Sing the song of redeeming love. (Alma 5:26)

The repetition of sound in these scriptures is exceptional! The following Book of Mormon sentences and phrases are also masterful.

> O that I were an angel. (Alma 29:1)
> Feast upon the words of Christ. (2 Nephi 32:3)
> When ye are in the service of your fellow beings ye are only in the service of your God. (Mosiah 2:17)

I give unto men weakness that they may be humble. (Ether 12:27)

Have ye received his image in your countenances? (Alma 5:14)

Behold, the time is at hand, and on this night shall the sign be given, and on the morrow come I into the world. (3 Nephi 1:13)

And by the power of the Holy Ghost ye may know the truth of all things. (Moroni 10:5)

Here are some examples from the Pearl of Great Price:

Worlds without number. (Moses 1:33)
This is my work and my glory. (Moses 1:39)
The noble and great ones. (Abraham 3:22)
I know not, save the Lord commanded me. (Moses 5:6)

All of these breathe with the music of heaven that imprints the truths they teach indelibly upon the heart. It is not only the words that make them so memorable but also the fluid way they glide softly through the mind. Few men have been able to write with the pen of heaven, but Tyndale and Joseph Smith were among them. As a final example, notice how both used various types of repetition (first word, first and last word, back-to-back words) to create memorable scriptural expressions.

Tyndale: "*Blessed* are the poor in spirit. . . . *Blessed* are they that mourn. . . . *Blessed* are the meek. . . . *Blessed* are the merciful" (Matthew 5:3–7; emphasis added).

Joseph Smith: "*I glory* in plainness; *I glory* in truth; *I glory* in my Jesus" (2 Nephi 33:6; emphasis added).

Tyndale: "When *I* was a *child, I* spake *as a child, I* understood *as a child, I* imagined *as a child*" (1 Corinthians 13:11; emphasis added).

Joseph Smith: "*We* talk of *Christ, we* rejoice in *Christ, we* preach of *Christ, we* prophesy of *Christ*" (2 Nephi 25:26; emphasis added).

Tyndale: "*My God, My God,* why hast thou forsaken me?" (Matthew 27:46; emphasis added).

Joseph Smith: "A Bible! A Bible! We have got a Bible" (2 Nephi 29:3; emphasis added).

Both also used the device of mixing the senses for a particular effect. Tyndale writes, "Ye have made the *savour of us stink* in the *sight* of Pharaoh" (Exodus 5:21; emphasis added). Joseph Smith counters with Alma's compelling question, "After ye have *tasted* this *light* is your knowledge perfect?" (Alma 32:35; emphasis added). Recognizing why certain combinations of words delight and move us produces gratitude for the craftsmanship displayed. It also confirms our faith, particularly in Joseph Smith, for he did not have the decade-plus university training granted Tyndale. He was unlearned yet produced genius equal to the best learning of the age. When we read the Book of Mormon or the Bible, we witness the mark of the same eternal mind operating through the natural genius of two chosen men amplified by a spiritual gift bestowed by the Holy Ghost.

A Quiet Giant

Worms saw the beginning of the German Reformation when a resolute monk braced himself, looked into his own soul, and said, "My conscience is captive to the Word of God. . . . Here I stand. I cannot do otherwise."[7] It was also home to the first stirrings of the English Reformation as an unassuming Oxford scholar of Greek packed neatly printed hand-sized New Testaments in preparation for their bootleg journey into England. The English lion would soon roar at the Italian pope, with a determined Henry VIII seeking an heir and demanding the annulment of his marriage to Catherine of Aragon in favor of the petite Anne Boleyn, but in the hum and hurry of Peter Schoeffer's print shop a quiet giant rose up, and the world was changed forever.

NOTES

1. Greenslade, *Work of William Tindale,* 99.
2. Duffield, *Work of William Tyndale,* 28; emphasis added.
3. Pirated editions produced later by Dutch printers were filled with errors but sold just as readily.
4. Mozley, *William Tyndale,* 67; emphasis added.
5. *Webster's Word Histories,* 27.
6. Mozley, *William Tyndale,* 104–5.
7. Bainton, *A Life of Martin Luther,* 185.

THE FIRES OF
ST. PAUL'S CROSS

𝔚𝔥𝔢𝔫 a thing speedeth not well, we borrow speech, and say, 'The bishop hath blessed it;' because that nothing speedeth well that they meddle withal. If the porridge be burned too, or the meat over roasted, we say, 'The bishop hath put his foot in the pot,' or, 'The bishop hath played the cook;' because the bishops burn whom they lust, and whosoever displeaseth them.

—WILLIAM TYNDALE, *THE FOUR SENSES OF SCRIPTURE*

"PESTIFEROUS AND MOST PERNICIOUS POISON"

On October 24, 1526, Bishop Cuthbert Tunstall, once the object of Tyndale's hopes, issued the following decree: "By the duty of our pastoral office we are bound diligently, with all our power, to foresee, provide for, root out, and put away, all those things which seem to tend to the peril and danger of our subjects, and specially the destruction of their souls! Wherefore, we having understanding, by the report of divers credible persons, and also by the evident appearance of the matter, that many children of iniquity . . . blinded through extreme wickedness, wandering from the way of truth and the Catholic faith, craftily have translated the New Testament into our English tongue, intermingling therewith many heretical articles and erroneous opinions, pernicious and offensive, seducing the simple people . . . containing, in the English tongue, that pestiferous and most pernicious poison, dispersed throughout all our diocese in great number."[1]

Tunstall then ordered that all biblical contraband be turned over for burning. He summoned London's booksellers, warning them not to bring into England any more heretical writings, and he charged the church's archdeacons to gather and turn in all such books within thirty days. In light of English hunger for Jesus' words in the mother tongue, the bishop's decree served more as an advertisement. Its sharp language indicates that only months after its completion, Tyndale's work was spreading rapidly throughout London. This was indeed distressing to the authorities, for where would it stop? On November 3, William Warham, archbishop of Canterbury, issued his own prohibition of Tyndale's New Testaments. Tunstall and his allies, including Thomas More and Cardinal Thomas Wolsey, with Henry's backing, were determined to meet the fire of the word with the fires of St. Paul.

Tunstall was a humanist thinker, a scholar of Greek, a friend of Erasmus, but he was so blinded by the gnats of his own prejudice that he could not see the camels of brilliance in Tyndale's work. Tunstall claimed the new translation had more than three thousand errors, and More insisted it had as many faults as the sea had shells. As the fate of history worked its ironic twists, within a few short years Tunstall would openly verify the greatness of Tyndale's work. At present, however, he failed to understand as pastor to his people the need to satisfy the hunger of a famished nation for a New Testament feast. The people felt the pangs of Amos's "famine in the land . . . of hearing the words of the Lord" and were running "to and fro to seek the word of the Lord" (Amos 8:11–12).

Tyndale penned a beautiful passage on the purpose of scripture. How different in spirit it reads from Tunstall's order, but how similar in spirit it reads to Lehi's description of the iron rod. "The scripture is that wherewith God draweth us unto him. . . . The scriptures spring out of God, and flow unto Christ, and were given to lead us to Christ. Thou must therefore go along by the scripture as by a line, until thou come at Christ, which is the way's end and resting place."[2]

CIRCLING THE FIRE

As early as February and March 1526, the first trickle of Tyndale's New Testaments had arrived and were selling in London. Care was needed to transport them from Worms to the shipping ports, with most of them departing from Antwerp for their journey across the English Channel. Roads were muddy, often impassable and unsafe. Searches and seizures occurred frequently. In the future, as publishing in city ports became less dangerous than overland transport or long river journeys from the interior, publications would be printed, hidden, and shipped from the same port city.

The religious atmosphere in England was already tense by October, when Tyndale's New Testaments were readily available. At Cambridge, Robert Barnes found himself in hot water over a sermon he had delivered the previous Christmas. He was summoned to London to appear before Cardinal Wolsey. Miles Coverdale, his good friend, courageously came with him. Given the choice between recanting and burning, he chose recantation but was sentenced with four German merchants of the London Steelyard to public humiliation.

On February 11, 1526, Barnes and the four merchants were ordered to carry the heretic's bundle of sticks on their backs while kneeling in the aisle of St. Paul's Cathedral as Bishop John Fisher delivered a brimstone sermon against them. Afterward, they stepped outside to St. Paul's Cross, where a huge bonfire was ignited. Attended by thousands and presided over by Cardinal Wolsey, who was seated upon a high scaffold surrounded by bishops, abbots, and priors, the offending men had to circle the fire three times and then throw their bundles of sticks into the flames. It was a warning that only the mercy of the church had saved them from being thrown into the fire themselves. If they were caught again with an English New Testament, the chains of the stake would encircle them. But the desire to teach was strong. How could men like Barnes stop themselves?

Great piles of forbidden books, particularly Luther's writings—some of which had been confiscated in Sir Thomas More's surprise search of the Steelyard in January 1526—were sacrificed to the flames, but an even more "pestiferous and most pernicious" enemy was sailing to England, concealed in the holds of ships. All the power of church and state mustered against this new foe would not be able to stop it.

As the months ticked by, New Testaments began arriving at alarming rates. Henry VIII entered the fray in 1527, writing, "We . . . with the deliberate advice of the most reverend fathers of the spirituality, have determined the said and untrue translations to be burned, with further sharp correction and punishment against the keepers and readers of the same."[3] The crimes of reading and keeping Bibles would be strictly enforced, resulting in "sharp correction and punishment" by order of his majesty.

As a result of Tunstall's and Warham's decrees, great numbers of Tyndale's New Testaments were publicly burned at St. Paul's Cross in the fall of 1526. Humphrey Monmouth, a personal friend and supporter of Tyndale, painfully witnessed the burning. Cardinal Campeggio, the papal representative, felt differently and wrote to Rome of this first public condemnation of Tyndale's translation, declaring that "no holocaust could be more pleasing to Almighty God."[4]

WILY TRADERS AND CLANDESTINE MEETINGS

Despite public conflagrations, desire continued for the New Testament's precious words and the profits that could be made by daring merchants and booksellers. The small pocket-sized octavo edition was easy to conceal, and sales increased. A wily trader could buy the books at the fairs of Frankfurt, Germany, or directly from the printer, knowing that a ready market waited if he could slip them past the ever-watchful eyes of Catholic sympathizers.

Almost every ship sailing between Antwerp and England contained some form of contraband. Smugglers landed their wares in dozens of inlets and tributaries along England's extended coastline. To reduce risks, they then used footpaths and muddy back roads.

Under King Henry's edicts, informers received large portions of the fines levied on those arrested. Spies on both sides of the law were common, and bribes induced community authorities to look the other way. New Testaments were reportedly sold in Coleman Street, Honey Lane, Hosier Lane, and in the private house of one Simon Fish. And, of course, there was always the narrow back alley or wayside path.

Tyndale hoped to keep the price of his Bibles affordable for the working classes, yet profits often reached as high as 500 percent. Even then, cost of the books was well within the reach of the majority of Henry's subjects.

With doors locked and lookouts posted, small groups of people gathered in clandestine meetings in the dead of night while one of their number read forbidden words in quiet tones. Families purchased the books, and parents softly taught their children from the smuggled texts. Wolsey, Tunstall, and More began serious surveillance, setting snares to catch the fishermen, tailors, and woolen merchants of London.

"We read, for example, of Thomas Geffrey, tailor; of John Medwall, a scrivener's servant; of Mathew Ward, a merchant adventurer; and of Robert Ward, a shoemaker by Fleet Street; all of whom were arrested and forced to recant their heretical beliefs."[5] Persecution was not limited to men. "All eight members of a family called Wily were arrested, including 'Lucy Wily, and Agnes Wily, two young girls.'"[6]

Oxford saw its share of arrests. After Thomas Garrett was caught slipping 350 books into the university, he was hauled before Cardinal Wolsey. He and several of his supporters were then thrown into a makeshift prison, where three of them died. Bonfires lit the streets of Oxford, and the procession of stick-carrying offenders grew.

Despite his recent memory of the heat from the bonfire's flames, Robert Barnes, who was under house arrest in an Augustinian friary, sold one of Tyndale's New Testaments to a group of Lollards for three shillings and two pence.[7] He then faked his suicide with a series of notes that sent his jailors to his supposed drowning spot while he escaped across the English Channel. Back in London, Humphrey Monmouth's house was searched as part of an official effort to ferret out members of the Christian Brethren.

Tunstall's humanity, however, restrained him. He was not a bishop who favored burning people alive, and so far punishment was limited to imprisonment, public carrying of bundles of sticks, and days in the stocks. But the punishment proved insufficient to deter the blacksmiths, farmers, weavers, and fullers from making their purchases. Sometimes several pooled their money to buy a single New Testament. So while the printers on the Continent set the type, inked it, and pressed prized words onto a waiting rag paper, the secret meetings continued.

THE BATTLEFRONT SHIFTS TO THE CONTINENT

Demand grew so high that in Antwerp pirated editions of Tyndale's work began to appear. They were often poorly done because the printers rarely spoke or read the English they were typesetting, but the New Testaments sold just as handsomely. Luther once complained that he could not recognize his own works when the publishing pirates had finished with them.

On November 21, 1526, Wolsey instructed the English ambassador to the Low Countries,[8] John Hackett, to take the war to the Continent and stop the flow at its source. Christopher van Endhoven, a printer of pirated copies, was caught with freshly printed Bibles and arrested. To Hackett's frustration, however, leaders in Antwerp had no mind to quickly punish the printer or burn his books. But books bought by Wolsey's agents were burned across the Channel and eventually in Antwerp as well. For protection, printers produced pirated and official editions under false names and locations. This practice became Tyndale's prime mode of operation.

In June 1528, Cardinal Wolsey demanded that the regent of the Low Countries arrest and extradite Tyndale, Roye, and Richard

Herman, an English merchant. Roye and Tyndale had already separated, and neither could be found. Herman, a citizen of Antwerp, was arrested and accused of helping Tyndale. His trial dragged on, but he was released at last because of a lack of evidence. He was expelled from the English House,[9] and his business was ruined. His cause was taken up later by no less than Anne Boleyn, who requested his reinstatement.

Other searchers were sent to Holland to purchase information concerning Tyndale's whereabouts. Back in England, More was busily asking for clues about his dress, habits, and appearance.

THE CHIEF BUYER OF BIBLES

Authorities concocted a plan to buy all of the editions firsthand and have them destroyed. The plan, however, was not well thought out and only served to encourage more printing. Foxe recorded an intriguing conversation regarding Bishop Tunstall's purchase of large quantities of New Testaments for burning:

"In short space after, it fortuned that George Constantine was apprehended by Sir Thomas More, who was then chancellor of England, as suspected of certain heresies. Master More asked of him, saying, 'Constantine! I would have thee be plain with me in one thing that I will ask; and I promise thee I will show thee favor in all other things whereof thou art accused. There is beyond the sea, Tyndale, Roye, and a great many of you: I know they cannot live without help. There are some that succor them with money; and thou, being one of them, hadst thy part thereof, and therefore knowest whence it came. I pray thee, tell me, who be they that help them thus?' 'My Lord,' quoth Constantine, 'I will tell you truly: it is the bishop of London that hath holpen us, for he hath bestowed among us a great deal of money upon New Testaments to burn them; and that hath been, and yet is, our only succor and comfort.' 'Now by my troth,' quoth More, 'I think even the same; for so much I told the bishop before he went about it.'"[10]

Despite Constantine's cavalier attitude, he cracked under More's interrogation. He had been caught distributing Tyndale's books in England, and he now revealed names of those involved in smuggling, including the sailors and secret marks placed on shipments concealing New Testaments. Arrests promptly followed, and the reformers received a timely lesson about the type of men they could take into their confidence.

In a letter drafted October 4, 1528, Hermann Rinck, the Cologne official who chased Tyndale up the Rhine to Worms, wrote to Cardinal Wolsey, reporting on his efforts to intercept English works bound for Britain and revealing smuggling techniques. "Unless I had learned of the matter and had interposed, the books were to have been bound and concealed in paper covers, packed in ten bundles, covered with flax, and at a suitable opportunity craftily and without suspicion transported across the sea to Scotland and England, there to be sold merely as blank paper."[11]

For about a year and a half, authorities burned books, issued ecclesiastical decrees, and appealed for help to officials on the Continent in an effort to stop Tyndale's "pernicious poison." But they were losing the battle, and the poison was spreading—with the assurance that hundreds, perhaps even thousands, of New Testaments had been distributed in England.

"EVERYWHERE AND NOWHERE"

Certainly the persecution and book burning distressed Tyndale. He was not translating to warm the clergy's hands at the bonfires. "Some man will ask," he wrote, "Why I take the labour to make this work, insomuch as they will burn it, seeing they burnt the gospel? I answer, In burning the new Testament they did none other thing than that I looked for: no more shall they do, if they burn me also, if it be God's will it shall be so. Nevertheless, in translating the New Testament I did my duty, and so do I now, and will do as much more as God hath ordained me to do."[12]

Tyndale's movements are difficult to trace during this time. Sir

Thomas More, after years of fruitless searching, wrote to Erasmus, calling Tyndale "our heretic who is in exile and seems to be everywhere and nowhere."[13] Tyndale's doctrinal treatises *The Parable of the Wicked Mammon* and *The Obedience of a Christian Man*, published in 1528, appeared to come from Marburg, Germany. The title pages stated that Hans Luft, a Wittenberg printer of Luther's works, had printed them in Marburg. But recent research and the examination of woodcuts and type reveal that the true printer was John Hoochstraten, and the printing was done in Antwerp.

Hoochstraten published under a number of pseudonyms, including the rather unimaginative "Adam Anomymous, Basel."[14] He published enough approved works under his own name to remain legitimate in the public eye and thus cover his printing of lucrative contraband, which became increasingly dangerous. In October 1531, an edict was issued in the Low Countries aimed at suppressing unwelcome publications. A printer could now "be branded with a red hot iron, and lose an eye or a hand at the discretion of the judge."[15] Hoochstraten was in no mind to be linked with a work that could bring wrath down on his head by foolishly attaching his name to Tyndale's efforts, but covertly he continued to work with the great reformer.

Antwerp most likely became Tyndale's central abode from this point on. It had an independent spirit, a well-established community of English merchants, good printers, easy access to English ports, and a nonchalant attitude toward heresy. Business was at the center of Antwerp thoughts. Tyndale was not the last English reformer to find sanctuary there. Miles Coverdale and John Rogers both drew upon the resources and protective attitude of the city. They were close friends of Tyndale and saw his dream to fulfillment after his death.

Undoubtedly, Tyndale moved frequently as the search for him intensified. He returned to Hamburg when the heat was high in Antwerp, but Antwerp was the ideal place both for printing and smuggling. Though German cities offered more safety, Tyndale would risk safety for Antwerp's amenities.

FORCE OR FAILURE

The end of 1527 demanded a new, more concerted offensive. Wolsey had Thomas Bilney arrested in Cambridge and delivered him to Bishop Tunstall. Thomas was a diminutive man nicknamed "Little Bilney." Foxe describes him as "given to good letters; and very fervent and studious in the Scriptures, as appeared in his sermons, his converting of sinners, his preaching at the lazar cots [homes for lepers], wrapping them in sheets, helping them of that they wanted . . . a preacher to the prisoners and comfortless; a great doer in Cambridge."[16]

Bilney was seen as a significant force in the new spirit of the times, but Tunstall was convinced he was heretical. He was placed in the Tower of London for a year, where he recanted twice before being released. Slowly, Tunstall was finding the clues he needed to break the secrecy surrounding the importation of the contraband books. By the end of 1528, his prisons bulged with offenders like Edward Freese, a painter who was imprisoned for painting scripture verses on cloth for an inn.[17] It became clear that more strident measures were demanded to deter such heretics. Without greater force, the battle would fail. And so the clouds in England turned black with storm, and lightning fell to enkindle the fires of Smithfield.

NOTES

1. Bobrick, *Wide As the Waters,* 106–7.
2. Greenslade, *Work of William Tindale,* 160.
3. Mozley, *William Tyndale,* 114.
4. Ibid., 117.
5. Ackroyd, *Life of Thomas More,* 277.
6. Daniell, *William Tyndale,* 179.
7. Ackroyd, *Life of Thomas More,* 247–48.

8. The area bordering on the North Sea, comprising the Netherlands, Belgium, and Luxembourg.

9. A section of the city set apart for English merchants.

10. Foxe, *Book of Martyrs*, 180–81.

11. Mozley, *William Tyndale*, 131.

12. Greenslade, *Work of William Tindale*, 100.

13. Campbell, *Erasmus, Tyndale, and More*, 202–3.

14. Daniell, *William Tyndale*, 156.

15. Mozley, *William Tyndale*, 124 n.

16. Foxe, *Acts and Monuments*, 4:620.

17. Ibid., 4:694–95.

"CAME CHRIST TO MAKE THE WORLD MORE BLIND?"

As we sometime in our dreams think we bear heavier than a millstone on our breasts; or when we dream, now and then, that we would run away for fear, our legs seem heavier than lead; even so is the spirit oppressed and overladen of the flesh through custom, that she struggleth and striveth to get up and break loose in vain; until the God of mercy, which heareth her groan through Jesus Christ, come and loose her with his power, and put his cross of tribulation on the back of the flesh, to keep her down, to minish her strength and to mortify her.

—WILLIAM TYNDALE, *EXPOSITION UPON THE V, VI, AND VII CHAPTERS OF MATTHEW*

THE PARABLE OF THE WICKED MAMMON

Tyndale's 1526 New Testament evoked the most serious attacks, but two of his treatises printed in 1528—*The Parable of the Wicked Mammon* and *The Obedience of a Christian Man*—also sparked condemnation. The title of the first comes from Christ's parable in Luke 16 about the unjust steward. Published on May 8, it echoes Luther's main tenet, the foundation doctrine of all Protestantism—that of justification by faith in the grace of Christ.

Tyndale circulated *The Parable of the Wicked Mammon* as a defense of faith in Christ as taught in the New Testament, especially in the writings of Paul. *The Parable of the Wicked Mammon* is not an argument against good works but rather a definition of the cause motivating them. Once a man accepts the redeeming mercy of Christ, his heart fills with the passion of faith, and righteousness flows naturally. This became the crux of Tyndale's personal creed.

BOOK OF MORMON DOCTRINE IN 1528

The Book of Mormon doctrine of the Atonement's power to work a "mighty change" of heart (Alma 5:14) can be found in *The Wicked Mammon.* Alma or King Benjamin could have written the following: "Therefore [faith] is . . . mighty in operation, full of virtue, and ever working; which also reneweth a man, and begetteth him afresh, altereth him, changeth him, and turneth him altogether into a new nature and conversation; so that a man feeleth his heart altogether altered and changed."[1] As Alma wrote, "Marvel not that all mankind . . . must be born again; yea, born of God, changed from their carnal and fallen state, to a state of righteousness, being redeemed of God . . . and thus they become new creatures" (Mosiah 27:25–26).

Other Nephite echoes abound in Tyndale's address to the new readers of holy writ. Moroni's counsel to "come unto Christ, and be perfected in him . . . and love God with all your might, mind and strength," and his promise that God's grace will then be "sufficient for you, that by his grace ye may be perfect in Christ . . . that ye become holy, without spot" (Moroni 10:32–33) resound in Tyndale's comforting words based on the same hope. "See therefore thou have God's promises in thine heart, and that thou believe them without wavering: and when temptation ariseth, and the devil layeth the law and thy deeds against thee, answer him with the promises; and turn to God. . . . Also remember, that his Son's blood is stronger than all the sins and wickedness of the whole world; and therewith quiet thyself, and thereunto commit thyself, and bless thyself in all temptation . . . with that holy candle."[2]

"If We Fall a Thousand Times in a Day"

The "infinite atonement" (Alma 34:12) taught by Amulek is tenderly announced by Tyndale, who encouraged his readers with the promise "that if through fragility we fall a thousand times in a day, yet if we do repent again, we have alway mercy laid up for us in store in Jesus Christ our Lord."[3] Mormon testifies that in the "meek and lowly in heart," charity is born of faith and leads a man to "lay hold upon every good thing" (Moroni 7:44, 19). In beautiful prose, Tyndale says the same: "Deeds are the fruits of love; and love is the fruit of faith. Love, and also the deeds, are great or small according to the proportion of faith. Where faith is mighty and strong, there is love fervent, and deeds plenteous, and done with exceeding meekness: where faith is weak, there is love cold, and the deeds few and seldom, as flowers and blossoms in winter."[4]

Alma taught his son Shiblon to "acknowledge your unworthiness before God at all times" and in that acknowledgment pray, "O Lord, forgive my unworthiness, and remember my brethren in mercy" (Alma 38:14). Tyndale wrote, "Faith, when she prayeth, setteth not her good deeds before her, saying, 'Lord, for my good deeds do this or that'; nor bargaineth with God, saying 'Lord, grant me this, or do this or that, and I will do this or that for thee.' . . . But she setteth her infirmities and her lack before her face, and God's promises, saying, 'Lord, for thy mercy and truth, which thou hast sworn, be merciful unto me.'"[5]

"Brewer, Baker, Tailor"

Tyndale's treatise found its way onto lists of prohibited books and was denounced by the leading bishops and by Sir Thomas More, who called it a "well-spring of wickedness."[6] Salvation through faith on Christ, independent of the Church's seven sacraments, was too strong a threat. However, Tyndale was not writing to the highly placed but to the everyday man "of whatsoever craft or occupation he be of, whether brewer, baker, tailor, victualler, merchant, or husbandman."[7]

He wrote, "God looketh not first on thy work as the world doth, as though the beautifulness of the work pleased him as it doth the world, or as though he had need of them. But God looketh first on thy heart . . . he looketh with what heart thou workest, and not what thou workest; how thou acceptest the degree that he hath put thee in, and not of what degree thou art, whether thou be an apostle or a shoemaker."[8]

Medieval society was divided into three categories: the nobility, who did the fighting; the clergy, who did the praying; and everybody else, who did the working. Not needing to work showed one's quality and importance in the community. The creation of a middle class based on trade was slowly changing this worldview. And here came Tyndale preaching the New Testament doctrine that each man labor as though his efforts were done for Christ (Ephesians 6:5–9; Colossians 3:22–24). This doctrine elevated all trades—from seamstress to chimney sweep—to service to God.

Serving God required the best that could be offered. Calvin strongly pushed this doctrine, which, in time, crossed the Atlantic to become the basis of the American work ethic, but Tyndale had published its essential points years before Calvin launched his theology in Geneva. Obviously, awakening the mind to the truth of scripture was going to have some society-changing effects.

THE OBEDIENCE OF A CHRISTIAN MAN

On October 2, 1528, *The Obedience of a Christian Man* issued from the Antwerp press of Hoochstraten, once again under the alias of Hans Luft of Marburg. The network that smuggled religious books was becoming increasingly efficient, as well as lucrative, and soon conversation in England turned toward Tyndale's latest attack on the status quo. Tyndale wrote *The Obedience of a Christian Man* in response to accusations leveled at him and his fellow reformers and to encourage those being persecuted for owning his New Testament.

Tyndale's opponents blamed the revolts occurring in Europe on the reformers. In Germany, peasants had risen, creating chaos and atrocities in many provinces until savagely put down. Rome was mercilessly sacked by Charles V's troops, many of whom were Protestants. In Wycliffe's days, Wat Tyler's Peasants' Revolt, a rebellion of the lower class against the nobility and clergy, was laid at the feet of that early reformer. Because the whole world order was being swept away by the foolishness of men like Tyndale, the church had to control who read and interpreted the Bible.

Tyndale asserted, to the contrary, that past and current crises were not caused by God's word in mother tongues but by abuses of the nobility and clergy. Tyndale was not, despite claims to the contrary, trying to stir up rebellion in England, especially against the king. But scripture taught obedience to God, not man. The removal of clerical immunity and influence in state affairs was necessary. In time, these ideas spread beyond the vision of Tyndale and led to the separation of church and state.

Discerning the Poison from the Honey

Tyndale stated eloquently that his translations were needed so that the very problems he was accused of creating could be prevented. The scriptures were the source from which all Christian virtue flowed. Why could not the world see the reasonableness of making them available to all? As in *The Wicked Mammon,* Tyndale derived his points from the scriptures themselves. To the argument that the English language was so rough that it could not handle the nobility of God's voice, he responded:

"All that the apostles preached, were no doubt preached in the mother tongue. Why then might they not be written in the mother tongue? . . . They will say it cannot be translated into our tongue, it is so rude. It is not so rude. . . . The Greek tongue agreeth more with the English than with the Latin. And the properties of the Hebrew tongue agreeth a thousand times more with the English than with the Latin."[9]

Common people needed the scriptures to protect them from falsehood and temptation. How could anyone, in conscience, take this safeguard away from them? True, they might at first stumble in understanding, but if taught to read the scriptures intelligently, even the most humble could find enlightenment therein. If the Holy Spirit could inspire the writer, the Holy Spirit could also enlighten the reader.

"I would have you teach them also the properties and manner of speakings of the scripture, and how to expound proverbs and similitudes [parables]," Tyndale wrote. "And then, if they go abroad and walk by the fields and meadows of all manner of doctors and philosophers, they could catch no harm: they should discern the poison from the honey, and bring home nothing but that which is wholesome."[10]

The thirteenth article of faith enjoins the Saints to seek the lovely and virtuous. Tyndale tells us exactly how to do that. When we immerse ourselves in the scriptures, they provide a standard by which we may judge everything—the art on our walls, the music in our stereos, the books on our shelves, and the movies on our televisions.

MANY COSTLY SCHOOLMASTERS

The purpose of the church was to teach God's children. Tyndale brought this point home in a way every laboring parent understood: "When a whole parish of us hire a schoolmaster to teach our children, what reason is it that we should be compelled to pay this schoolmaster his wages . . . and to leave our children untaught? . . . Have we not given our tithes of courtesy unto one, for to teach us God's word[?] . . . And thus are we never taught, and are yet nevertheless compelled; yea, compelled to hire many costly schoolmasters."[11]

Tyndale could be sarcastic if the occasion required. Many a poor man knew the truth of the following: "The parson sheareth, the vicar shaveth, the parish priest polleth, the friar scrapeth and the pardoner pareth. We lack but a butcher to pull off the skin."[12] Considering that Cardinal Thomas Wolsey may have been a butcher's son, the hint was sure to be grasped.

A compromise solution would be to teach the priests so that they could teach the lay members. "But, alas!" many of them knew "no more what the new or old Testament meaneth, than do the Turks," Tyndale observed.[13] If they had English Bibles, however, they could "teach them the testament and promises which God hath made unto us in Christ, and how much he loveth us in Christ; and teach them the principles and the ground of the faith, and what the sacraments signify: *and then shall the Spirit work with thy preaching, and make them feel.*"[14]

This last phrase is typical Tyndale, the perfect expression of his thoughts in a short, pithy, moving sentence. Such a sentence could have come from the mind of Nephi, who testified: "When a man speaketh by the power of the Holy Ghost the power of the Holy Ghost carrieth it unto the hearts of the children of men" (2 Nephi 33:1).

"Hath He Not Made the English Tongue?"

Tyndale had little hope that the church would teach the plain text of the Testaments. Was there no recourse for the weaver and the cobbler? He believed there was and that God would provide it. He wrote, "If any man thirst for the truth, and read the scripture by himself, desiring God to open the door of knowledge unto him, God for his truth's sake will and must teach him."[15] Tyndale also wrote, "One scripture will help to declare another. And the circumstances, that is to say, the places that go before and after, will give light unto the middle text."[16]

All depended on an English text accessible to the layman. Quoting Psalms in a message to the clergy, Tyndale wrote: "'Happy are they which search the testimonies of the Lord.' . . . But how shall

I that do, when ye will not let me have his testimonies, or witnesses, in a tongue which I understand? Will ye resist God? Will ye forbid him to give his Spirit unto the lay as well as unto you? Hath he not made the English tongue? Why forbid ye him to speak in the English tongue then, as well as in the Latin?"[17]

Two millennia before Tyndale penned those questions, the Lord inspired Nephi to engrave similar queries regarding the translation of the Book of Mormon. "Wherefore murmur ye because that ye shall receive more of my word?. . . . I speak forth my words according to mine own pleasure. And because I have spoken one word ye need not suppose that I cannot speak another" (2 Nephi 29:8–9). The same spirit operated in both men. Even the cadence of each passage corresponds. While the world awaited visits from Moroni, God had not left mankind untutored.

Tyndale's ability to dive to the heart of a matter with trenchant questions is seen throughout *The Obedience.* Hinting at his full translating aspirations, which included the Old Testament, he cut a new swath through his opponents with each succeeding inquiry. "What is the cause that we may not have the old Testament, with the new also, which is the light of the old. . . ? *Came Christ to make the world more blind?"*[18]

FIRST TEACHER OF CIVIL DISOBEDIENCE

Tyndale knew the people would remain in darkness as long as the king felt threatened by the Bible's publication. His thought now turned to the matter of obedience. Subjects were bound by God's law to obey the civil powers that were accountable to God.

"All rulers . . . wield an authority from God, and must be obeyed. At the head of all stands the king, who has no superior. . . . Though kings are supreme, they may not rule as they list. They are servants of their people, and must treat every man, no matter how humble, as a brother. . . . Let kings do their duty to the people, and rule their own kingdom; let them put the priests to their own proper work, strip them of their worldly honours and riches, and set good laymen in the chief offices of state. . . . Let the king rule in fact as well as in name, and decide his own matters."[19]

Tyndale was arguing in favor of separation of church and state. Considering the difficulties Henry VIII would have with Pope Clement VII over his divorce from Catherine, these were provocative words indeed.

What if the man proved to be a tyrant? "What then is the duty of the Christian in this terror? He must disobey ungodly commands, but he must never resist by force," Tyndale counseled.[20] Rebellion brought chaos! All resistance must be passive. If resistance brought punishment, it was to be borne with meekness and a peaceful heart. Tyndale taught civil disobedience in the spirit of Henry David Thoreau and Gandhi. Much in *The Obedience of a Christian Man* harmonizes perfectly with statements about government in section 134 of the Doctrine and Covenants and in the twelfth article of faith.

In one of the great ironies of history, Sir Thomas More, who accused Tyndale of disloyalty and rebellion against the king, later did exactly what Tyndale suggested when Henry VIII pressured him to compromise his own conscience. More remained quietly resistant until his own martyrdom.

AN ALLY IN ANNE BOLEYN

At the time *The Obedience of a Christian Man* was published, Henry was enamored with Anne Boleyn. Anne was raised in France, where she learned all the graces that held Henry captivated and yet at bay for six long years while the wrangling over his divorce dragged on. She was influenced by the French humanists and looked favorably upon the reforming spirit. Her deluxe copy of Tyndale's 1534 New Testament, complete with the words *Anna Regina Angliae* (Anne, Queen of England) inscribed on the gold leaf edge of the pages, is in the British Library. The book is believed to have been a gift from Richard Herman, the Antwerp merchant whom Anne helped. Henry learned of the existence of *The Obedience* through Anne, who owned a copy.

Anne Boleyn.

Anne lent *The Obedience* to Anne Gainford, one of her gentle-women, who was being courted by George Zouch. In jest he snatched the book from her hand and began to read. He was so entranced with it that, despite her pleading, he took it to read further. As chance would have it, the dean of the king's chapel, a Dr. Sampson, noticed Zouch reading during a service and demanded he turn the book over. Everyone was on the lookout for contraband from the Continent. Delighted with his discovery, the dean went straight to Cardinal Wolsey, who in turn went to the king.

Anne was not popular with certain parties, and possession of a copy of *The Obedience* could, perhaps, lead to her downfall. Wolsey misjudged his influence, which was waning because of his failure to produce the coveted annulment of Henry's first marriage. In the interlude, Anne Boleyn asked Anne Gainford for her book, whereupon Anne fell on her knees, confessing that a young man had taken it from her and had lost it to the dean of the king's chapel, who had subsequently turned it over to Cardinal Wolsey.

"The Lady Anne shewed herself not sorry, nor angry with either of the two. But, said she, well, it shall be the dearest book that ever the dean or cardinal took away. The noble woman goes to the king, and upon her knees she desireth the king's help for her book. Upon the king's token the book was restored. And now bringing the book to him, she besought his grace most tenderly to read it. The king did so, and delighted in the book. For, saith he, this is a book for me and all kings to read."[21]

The Obedience of a Christian Man continued to be proscribed nevertheless, but Henry could not have failed to interpret it in a manner favorable to himself. How much it stimulated subsequent events is a matter of sharp debate. It is true, however, that in time Henry would limit the clergy to religious matters and confiscate much of their wealth and property—but by that time Tyndale would be dead.

WOLSEY'S FALL

Cardinal Wolsey's own season was running out. The great worldly prelate fell from the king's favor in the summer of 1528 to be replaced as chancellor by Sir Thomas More in October 1529. In another irony of history, Tyndale had suggested that the high office of chancellor be held by a layman, not by a clergyman. More fit the description, but religious zeal burned even hotter in him than it had in the great cardinal. Sir Thomas's assessment of his predecessor should have been a lesson for himself, but sermons are always easier to preach to the pews than to the man in the pulpit. "Glorious was he," More said, "very far above all measure, and that was the great pity, for it did him harm and made him abuse many great gifts that God had given him."[22]

In More and in John Stokesley, soon to be appointed new bishop of London, Tyndale would come up against his most bitter enemies. Sir Thomas More, like Wolsey, would "abuse his many great gifts." Persecution for those who possessed Tyndale's translations or other writings would not be quenched until the fires of England devoured a more precious fuel than books.

NOTES

1. Greenslade, *Work of William Tindale*, 170–71.
2. Ibid., 168.
3. Ibid., 170.
4. Ibid., 172–73.
5. Ibid., 175.
6. More, *Complete Works of St. Thomas More*, 6:i, 291, 424, in Daniell, *William Tyndale*, 170.
7. Greenslade, *Work of William Tindale*, 175.
8. Ibid., 174.
9. Ibid., 89.
10. Ibid., 91.
11. Ibid., 130.
12. Daniell, *William Tyndale*, 225.

13. Duffield, *Work of William Tyndale*, 325.
14. Ibid., 329; emphasis added.
15. Ibid.
16. Daniell, *William Tyndale*, 236.
17. Duffield, *Work of William Tyndale*, 331.
18. Ibid., 324; emphasis added.
19. Mozley, *William Tyndale*, 137–38.
20. Ibid., 138.
21. Ibid., 142–43.
22. Campbell, *Erasmus, Tyndale, and More*, 175.

"UNTO THE WORLD'S END"

Christ is the cause why I love thee, why I am ready to do the uttermost of my power for thee, and why I pray for thee. And as long as the cause abideth, so long lasteth the effect; even as it is always day so long as the sun shineth. Do therefore the worst thou canst unto me, take away my goods, take away my good name; yet as long as Christ remaineth in my heart, so long I love thee not a whit the less, and so long art thou as dear unto me as mine own soul, and so long am I ready to do thee good for thine evil and so long I pray for thee with all my heart: for Christ desireth it of me, and hath deserved it of me. Thine unkindness compared unto his kindness is nothing at all; yea, it is swallowed up as a little smoke of a mighty wind, and is no more seen or thought upon.

—WILLIAM TYNDALE, *THE OBEDIENCE OF A CHRISTIAN MAN*

"LET HIS LITTLE FLOCK BE BOLD"

The year 1528 was a time of natural disasters. Harvests were meager, and bread cost dearly. The summer saw a resurgence of the plague and the "sweating sickness." Henry VIII fled London for the countryside, while Sir Thomas More blamed England's woes on William Tyndale, certain the cause of "the lack of corn and cattle" was a "sore punishment" from God "for the receipt of these pestilent books of heresy."[1] Bishop Cuthbert Tunstall and the man who would replace him in 1530, John Stokesley, shared

More's assessment. Stokesley had known Tyndale at Oxford, serving as vice president of Magdalen Hall when Tyndale was a student.

Persecution mounted under More and Stokesley even as the king warmed to the ideas of *The Obedience of a Christian Man.* However, a council of church leaders convinced the king that Bible translations were dangerous for the realm, and Henry supported their destruction.

So far only books had been destroyed, but in February 1530 Thomas Hitton was burned at Maidstone. The overseas reformers were stunned. Foxe records that Hitton "was a preacher . . . whom the bishop of Canterbury, William Warham, and Fisher, bishop of Rochester, after they had long kept him in prison, and tormented him with sundry torments, and that he notwithstanding continued constant; at last they burned him at Maidstone, for the constant and manifest testimony of Jesus Christ."[2]

Hitton was an ally of Tyndale, a runner who carried correspondence across the Channel. He had recently been on the Continent, and he confessed to his examiners that he had smuggled a New Testament into England. His capture was all the more tragic because he was mistaken for a common thief who had stolen some linen drying on a hedge. The real thief escaped, but More reported that Hitton was captured with "certain letters secretly conveyed in his coat, written from evangelical brethren here unto the evangelical heretics beyond the sea."

Sir Thomas called Hitton "the devil's stinking martyr" who "learned the great part of Tyndale's holy books; and now the spirit of error and lying hath taken his wretched soul with him straight from the short fire to the fire eternal."[3] More showed intelligence and nobility throughout his life, but with perceived heretics, the warmth of his compassion was drenched cold and the bright flame of an otherwise Christian soul turned to ash.

Hitton was the first English martyr for Tyndale, and his death stung the reformer sharply. He mentioned Hitton several times in later writings. It was one thing to suffer exile and persecution for oneself, another to know that friends whom he had influenced were suffering painful deaths. Perhaps Tyndale felt that suffering was inevitable, for he had written beautiful words of comfort and reassurance in *The Obedience of a Christian Man.* Had they echoed in Hitton's ears as the flames engulfed him?

"Let it not make thee despair, neither yet discourage thee, O reader, that it is forbidden thee in pain of life and goods, or that it is made breaking of the king's peace, or treason unto his highness, to read the word of thy soul's health; but much rather be bold in the Lord, and comfort thy soul. . . . Christ is with us unto the world's end. Let his little flock be bold therefore: for if God be on our side, what matter maketh it who be against us, be they bishops, cardinals, popes, or whatsoever names they will?"[4]

Would not the Savior comfort Joseph Smith and Oliver Cowdery in the midst of persecution with similar words? "Fear not, little flock; do good; let earth and hell combine against you, for if ye are built upon my rock, they cannot prevail" (D&C 6:34).

THOMAS BILNEY—"WHEN THOU WALKEST IN THE FIRE"

With all his persecuting zeal, Bishop Tunstall stopped short of sending men to the stake. Bishop Stokesley saw things differently, and More was his confederate. Early in 1531, Thomas Bilney and Richard Bayfield were arrested for the second time. Both were among the Cambridge scholars. Bilney had been examined for heresy in 1527, kept in the Tower of London for a year, and recanted. His conscience had gnawed at him ever since, and he "took such repentance and sorrow, that he was near the point of utter despair . . . for he thought that all the whole Scriptures were against him, and sounded to his condemnation."[5]

In 1531, Bilney could bear the torment no longer, made his decision, and told friends "that he would go to Jerusalem," alluding to Christ's resolve to meet his death at the hands of his enemies.

Thomas Bilney plucked from the pulpit.

Leaving Cambridge, he was soon evangelizing in the open air, teaching the English Bible, and challenging Catholic doctrine. In Norwich, he gave an "anchoress . . . a New Testament of Tyndale's translation, and *The Obedience of a Christian Man;* whereupon he was apprehended and carried to prison."[6]

Bilney was examined, condemned, and removed from the priesthood. The night before his execution, while sitting with friends who came to comfort him, he put "his hand toward the flame of the candle burning before them, . . . and feeling the heat thereof" he quoted Isaiah: "When thou walkest in the fire, it shall not burn thee, and the flame shall not kindle upon thee, for I am the Lord thy God, the holy One of Israel, thy Saviour."[7]

The next day, Bilney was taken to a valley called the Lollard's Pit, which afforded a good view for the people. He was chained to the stake, the words *fiat justitia* (let justice be done) were called out, and the fire was lit. At first the contrary wind blew the flames away from him, prolonging his agony. In his pain, Bilney softly called "Jesus!" over and over until the fire grew strong enough to end his life.

RICHARD BAYFIELD—THE PRICE OF SMUGGLING

Richard Bayfield was a monk who had been converted to reform by Robert Barnes through the instrumentality of Tyndale's New Testament and his two famous treatises. He began preaching openly, which led to his imprisonment. In prison, he was "sore whipped, with a gag in his mouth, and then stocked." Upon his release, he too became a courier for Tyndale. Bayfield "mightily prospered in the knowledge of God, and was beneficial to Master Tyndale, and Master Frith; for he brought substance with him, and was their own hand, and sold all their works."[8]

Smuggling was dangerous but effective. Tyndale's books were moving beyond the merchant and learned circles and into the hands of the laboring man. Forbidden works were hidden in bales of cloth with secret marks known only to the smugglers. "Barrels or casks, apparently full of wine or oil, might secrete water-tight boxes holding dangerous propaganda," F. C. Avis writes. "Cargoes of wheat or grain, hides or skins were not always made up exclusively of these items. Flour sacks often held carefully packed contraband books strategically placed in the meal. Chests with false sides or bases, hidden receptacles or secret compartments brought over documents."[9]

George Constantine, whom More had apprehended and grilled for information, betrayed Bayfield. Hunted down, his hiding places diminishing, Bayfield was finally caught at his bookbinder's house. During his inquest, he confessed that he had brought books into England, landing them at Colchester, St. Catharine's Point, and Norfolk. Bayfield was no fool, trying to change his entry point with each new shipment. The last were transported to London "in a mail."

Bayfield was sentenced as a relapsed heretic and was shackled in the Tower by his neck, waist, and legs. On the day of his execution, he was publicly "degraded," or stripped of his priesthood. Bishop Stokesley "took his crosier-staff, and smote him on the breast, that he threw him down backwards." Since canon law forbade the church from putting any man to death, prisoners were turned over to civil jurisdiction for punishment. It was a technicality but eased the conscience and left the church without blood on its hands. Bayfield was carried to Newgate, where he suffered a painful death "for lack of a speedy fire."[10]

Constantine was allowed to escape from More's stocks at Chelsea, a London borough located along the Thames River. Authorities undoubtedly followed him back to Antwerp, hoping he might lead them to Tyndale. But the translator's network was effective, and he eluded Constantine from that time forth as a false brother. Sir Thomas More, triumphant once again over Tyndale, could not resist another painful jab at his arch foe, reminding him, "Of Bayfield's burning hath Tyndale no great cause to glory."[11]

John Tewkesbury—A Common Leather Seller

"Who will be next?" must have crossed Tyndale's mind many times, as did the gnawing concern that he was in large measure responsible for the suffering of his friends. Yet, he sensed from the beginning the offering required. In *The Obedience of a Christian Man,* he warned the faithful of the trials to come. "If the king, at the bidding of the bishops, makes bible-reading a treason against the state, and punishes it with prison and the fire, the true believer will stand firm, and suffer every penalty for Christ's sake."[12] Among the true believers were common craftsmen.

John Tewkesbury, a London leather seller, was taken before Bishop Tunstall in 1529 for possessing Tyndale's Testament and *The Parable of the Wicked Mammon,* but "he was very expert and prompt in his answers, in such sort that [Tunstall], and all his learned men, were ashamed that a leather-seller should so dispute with them, with such power of the Scriptures and heavenly wisdom, that they were not able to resist him." Taken to Chelsea, More's home, Tewkesbury was put in the stocks for six days before being "racked in the Tower till he was almost lame."[13] Finally he abjured.

For penance he was required to carry a bundle of sticks in St. Paul's Church and to stand with the bundle at St. Paul's Cross on Sunday, at Newgate Market and Cheapside the following Wednesday, and at St. Peter's Church in Cornhill and the market of Leadenhall on Friday. For the rest of his life, Tewkesbury was to wear patches featuring embroidered sticks, "one on his left sleeve, and the other on his right sleeve."[14]

Watching Richard Bayfield's courage had strengthened Tewkesbury's own courage. He was soon accused again of possessing Tyndale's works, believing in justification by faith, denying purgatory, and rejecting the literal presence of Christ's body and blood in the sacrament. Further, he had removed the patches from his sleeves. Only one fate awaited relapsed heretics. More and Stokesley had him burned in Smithfield, a district in northwestern London, just before Christmas 1531. Again, Sir Thomas could not conceal his glee. The poor leather seller had been "burned as there was never wretch I [deemed] better worthy." Tewkesbury was now in hell, "an hot firebrand burning at his back, that all the water in the world will never be able to quench."[15]

JAMES BAINHAM—TEARS IN A CHURCH PEW

More and Stokesley were not afraid to go after higher game than leather sellers and relapsed monks. James Bainham was a "gentleman, son to one Master Bainham, a knight of Gloucestershire . . . an earnest reader of Scriptures." More took him to Chelsea for interrogation and then sent him to the Tower to be racked. After refusing More's demands to "accuse the gentlemen . . . of his acquaintance" or "show where his books lay," he was sent to the Tower. His wife "was sent to the Fleet [a prison], and their goods confiscated."[16] But Bainham was made of sterner stuff than the betraying Constantine. More could not squeeze from him the names of his believing friends.

Brought before Stokesley, he was arraigned, among other religious crimes, "for his books of Scripture, and for his judgment of Tyndale . . . he had the New Testament translated into the English tongue by Tyndale within this month, and thought he offended not God in using and keeping the same, notwithstanding that he knew the king's proclamation to the contrary, and that it was prohibited in the name of the church, at Paul's Cross; but, for all that, he thought the word of God had not forbid it. Confessing moreover, that he had in his keeping within this month these books: *The Parable of the Wicked Mammon, The Obedience of a Christian Man.* . . . In all these books he never saw any errors. . . . And as concerning the New Testament in English, he thought it utterly good, and that the people should have it as it is. Neither did he ever know that Tyndale was a naughty fellow."[17]

When asked if he knew anyone who had lived a true Christian life, "he said he knew Bayfield and thought that he died in the true faith of Christ."[18] This was the last straw, and though of the nobility,

Bainham had no hope unless he recanted. After continual interrogation, he wavered and then broke, agreeing to deny his past beliefs and conform to the Catholic faith. "I will," he said, "forsake all my articles, and will meddle no more with them."[19] For his penance the next Sunday, he carried a bundle of sticks on his shoulder at St. Paul's Cross while the sermon was preached. After paying a twenty-pound fine to the king, he was released and sent home.

Like Thomas Bilney, Bainham was tortured by his conscience. A month later, unable to bear his guilt, he confessed his weakness to all he knew and asked for forgiveness. He then made peace with fellow believers "in a warehouse in Bow-Lane," where they met in secret. The next Sunday he took Tyndale's New Testament in his hand, placed *The Obedience of a Christian Man* next to his heart, and walked into St. Austin's Church. He "stood up . . . before the people in his pew, there declaring openly, with weeping tears, that he had denied God; and prayed all the people to forgive him, and to beware of his weakness, and not to do as he did." Not content with a public admission, which alone doomed him to the fire, "he wrote also certain letters to the bishop, to his brother, and to others; so that shortly after he was apprehended, and so committed to the Tower of London."[20]

The Best Blood of the Sixteenth Century

Tyndale had written in the book Bainham carried with him into St. Austin's that Sunday morning heartening, empathetic words to all who, out of fear of the heretic's stake, had denied their beliefs and struggled with guilt. The words must have rung in Bainham's ears as he stood there weeping in his pew with Tyndale's New Testament freely displayed in his hand:

"Tribulation for righteousness is not a blessing only, but also a gift, that God giveth unto none save his special friends. . . . Let thy care be to prepare thyself with all thy strength, for to walk which way he will have thee, and to believe that he will go with thee and assist thee, and strengthen thee against all tyrants, and deliver thee out of all tribulation. But what way or by what means he will do it, that commit unto him and his godly pleasure and wisdom, and cast that care upon him. . . . If any man clean against his heart, but overcome with the weakness of the flesh, for fear of persecution have denied, as Peter did, or have delivered [to the bishops] his book [the Bible] or put it away secretly, let him, if he repent, come again, and take better hold, and not despair. Through such failures we learn to trust not in ourselves but in God, whose work alone can endure in the fire of tribulation."[21]

Bainham went to the bonfire of Smithfield on the last day of April 1531. Just before his death he addressed the crowd: "I am come hither, good people! accused and condemned for an heretic, Sir Thomas More being both my accuser and my judge: and these be the articles that I die for, which be a very truth, and grounded on God's word, and no heresy. . . . *I say it is lawful for every man and woman, to have God's book in their mother tongue.*" As the flames shot up and engulfed him, he cried out to his tormentors, "I feel no more pain . . . but it is to me as a bed of roses."[22]

When Nephi was carried away by the Spirit in vision, did he know the price men would pay to read the book that he saw "was carried forth among them"—the book that was "of great worth unto the Gentiles"? (1 Nephi 13:20, 23). The "Book of Mormon and [the] . . . Doctrine and Covenants of the church, cost the best blood of the nineteenth century to bring them forth for the salvation of a ruined world" (D&C 135:6). In like manner, the Bible cost the best blood of the sixteenth century.

Notes

1. Ackroyd, *Life of Thomas More,* 278; spelling standardized.
2. Foxe, *Acts and Monuments,* 4:619.
3. Mozley, *William Tyndale,* 228–29.
4. Ibid., 135.
5. Foxe, *Acts and Monuments,* 4:641.

6. Ibid., 4:642; an anchoress is a woman who lives in solitude for religious reasons.

7. Ibid., 4:652–53.

8. Ibid., 4:681.

9. As quoted in Daniell, *William Tyndale,* 186.

10. Foxe, *Acts and Monuments,* 4:687–88.

11. More, *Complete Works of St. Thomas More,* 8: Part 1, 17.

12. Mozley, *William Tyndale,* 138.

13. Foxe, *Acts and Monuments,* 4:688–89.

14. Ibid., 4:692.

15. Ackroyd, *Life of Thomas More,* 305.

16. Foxe, *Acts and Monuments,* 4:697–98.

17. Ibid., 4:699–700. In Tyndale's time, "naughty" was used to describe an immoral, wicked, or rude person, not a mischievous child (*Webster's Word Histories,* 316).

18. Ibid., 4:699.

19. Ibid., 4:701.

20. Ibid., 4:702.

21. Mozley, *William Tyndale,* 135.

22. Foxe, *Acts and Monuments,* 4:704–5.

SHIPWRECK AND JEHOVAH

𝔗his is a book worthy to be read in day and night and never to be out of hands. . . . Herein also thou mayest learn right meditation or contemplation, which is nothing else save the calling to mind and a repeating in the heart of the wonderful deeds of God.

—WILLIAM TYNDALE, "PROLOGUE TO DEUTERONOMY"

LOST LABORS

Part of the fury directed at the English reformers in 1530 lay in Tyndale's newest publication. As if the New Testament was not serious enough, Tyndale's Pentateuch, the first five books of the Old Testament, began to make its way through the wharves and warehouses of English ports and into the hands of eager purchasers. The stories of the New Testament were somewhat familiar to the people, but here was the drama of God's first dealings with men unveiled in gripping English. It was new and exciting, and the scripture-hungry population took to it with a vigor that could still be heard in the pulpit-pounding sermons of American evangelicals centuries later.

Tyndale, who could not have had even the most elementary knowledge of Hebrew when he fled England, somehow found time in the midst of all his other endeavors to vanquish the language of the Old Testament. Hebrew teachers lived in Wittenberg, Hamburg, Marburg, and Worms—cities associated with Tyndale's movements.

Once he learned Hebrew's basic elements, his own natural gifts took over, and he honed his skill with private study.

The Pentateuch was printed in January 1530 in Antwerp. It was the first scriptural translation directly from Hebrew into English. Tyndale's accomplishment generates even greater appreciation when we realize that he lost his original translation of the Old Testament's first five books in a shipwreck and had to start over. The experience was perhaps not quite as agonizing as Joseph Smith's loss of the first 116 pages of his Book of Mormon translation, but it was certainly painful to Tyndale, who had labored long and hard.

By 1529, with English authorities closing in, it was time to move and let the hounds bay in an empty city for a while. Edicts had been issued that could quickly end Tyndale's work as well as his life, even in Antwerp. Though the city fathers generally looked the other way, foreign pressure from England was growing. For Tyndale, movement was effective and necessary, but his move from Antwerp cost him dearly.

"Satan, the prince of darkness, maligning the happy course and success of the gospel, set to his might also, how to impeach and hinder the blessed travails of that man; as by this, and also by sundry other ways may appear," Foxe writes. "For at what time Tyndale had translated the fifth book of Moses called Deuteronomy, minding to print the same at Hamburgh, he sailed thitherward [from Antwerp]; where by the way, upon the coast of Holland, he suffered shipwreck, by which he lost all his books, writings and copies, and so was compelled to begin all again anew, to his hindrance, and doubling of his labours. Thus, having lost by that ship, both money, his copies, and his time, he came in another ship to Hamburgh, where, at his appointment, Master Coverdale tarried for him, and helped him in the translating of the whole five books of Moses, from Easter till December, in the house of a worshipful widow, Mistress Margaret von Emerson, A.D. 1529."[1]

Since it took the good part of a year to retranslate Genesis through Deuteronomy, Tyndale must have labored on the lost manuscript for much of 1528 and early 1529. His understanding of Hebrew was indeed phenomenal. Considering that Tyndale was martyred before he could translate the poetic and prophetic books of the Old Testament, the lost year is tragic. What would we give to have Tyndale's Psalms or Isaiah? Yet character is forged in the fire of adversity and disappointment, and Tyndale doggedly began the difficult process with his new helper, Miles Coverdale.

A NEW SCRIBE

In Hamburg, Tyndale needed new funds and new books, including the Septuagint (the Greek translation of the Old Testament) and Martin Luther's German translation. Hamburg was a newly won member of the German Reformation and was, therefore, safe. Tyndale had a home at the widow von Emerson's, a trusted and competent friend awaiting him in Miles Coverdale, and access to a good printer, George Richolff, son of a well-known printer from Lubeck.[2]

Coverdale, a former monk, was forty-two at the time. Tyndale must have formed his friendship with him at Cambridge, where he was a scholar. Coverdale, rather than meet the fate of Thomas Bilney and Richard Bayfield, fled England when he was suspected of preaching against such Catholic practices as the confessional and the mass. It is almost certain he went to Hamburg at Tyndale's request and could have been the man Tyndale initially wanted instead of William Roye.

By the time Tyndale had finished his second translation of the Pentateuch, Cardinal Thomas Wolsey had fallen from power in England. Henry VIII was increasingly frustrated with the church, asking for the support of the universities and expecting it from his new chancellor, Thomas More. With England's attention drawn elsewhere, Tyndale felt he could return to Antwerp for the printing with Hoochstraten. Antwerp was more dangerous than Hamburg, but its easy access to the English Channel and English ports made it more convenient for smuggling. Tyndale was not one to compromise his work by overanxiety about his own safety. Coverdale, who stayed in Germany and became a schoolmaster, would later play a major role in fulfilling Tyndale's dream.

MORE BOOKS TO BURN

Printed under cover of Hans Luft at Marburg, Tyndale's Pentateuch translation began to appear in England as a hand-sized book. Now the great stories of Genesis and Exodus found a home in Tyndale's poetic English: "In the beginning God created heaven and earth. The earth was void and empty, and darkness was upon the deep, and the spirit of God moved upon the water. Then God said: let there be light and there was light."[3] God's light had found its way to the commoner, though Tyndale's new achievement was hunted and burned as relentlessly as his New Testament. Today only a mere half-dozen or so copies remain.

Each of the Pentateuch's five books had its own prologue, so they could be circulated separately. Three of the books were printed in a different type, suggesting that Tyndale and Hoochstraten may have used two presses concurrently to expedite the process. Having lost his first translation, Tyndale likely wanted his new translation out as soon as possible. The printer also had compelling reasons to finish the run and quickly dispense with incriminating evidence.

In the Pentateuch, Tyndale continued to create a dialect of faith—a scriptural diction with speech patterns used even today. But he was not writing to impress. His language was not affected, and it contained no ostentation. He did not try to impose himself in his work. Unconscious of his own presence behind the words, he rendered holy writ into a message all could appreciate. In this he was like Joseph Smith, who also avoided writing for effect.[4]

Hebrew lent itself well to English speech and Tyndale's personal style. He favored single-syllable words and phrases dominated by them, which slows the reader down. Scripture is meant to be searched and must be read slowly, allowing time for reflection. Today we read things too quickly, and our sentence structure and use of polysyllabic words hurries us along from thought to thought.

A PRECIOUS JEWEL

A master scriptorian, Tyndale counseled his readers in the prologue of the Pentateuch how to read scripture:

"Though a man had a precious jewel and a rich, yet if he wist not the value thereof nor wherefore it served, he were neither the better nor richer of a straw. Even so though we read the scripture and babble of it never so much, yet if we know not the use of it, and wherefore it was given, and what is therein to be sought, it profiteth us nothing at all. It is not enough therefore to read and talk of it only, but we must also desire God day and night instantly to open our eyes, and to make us understand and feel wherefore the scripture was given, that we may apply the medicine of the scripture, every man to his own sores. . . . As thou readest therefore think that every syllable pertaineth to thine own self, and suck out the pith of the scripture, and arm thyself against all assaults. . . . For their learning and comfort, is the fruit of the scripture and cause why it was written. And with such a purpose to read it, is the way to everlasting life."[5]

Part of the precious nature of Tyndale's newest jewel lay in the manner in which he adapted Hebrew structures into English. In *The Obedience*, Tyndale noted that Hebrew went into English a thousand times better than it went into Latin. He was true to the Hebrew, and the English language was enriched by its syntax. His faithfulness to Hebrew created, among other things, the construct noun phrase. He gave us "the book of Moses" instead of "Moses' Book," "the children of Israel" rather than "Israel's children," "the hand of the Lord" instead of "the Lord's hand."

The noun phrase consists of noun + of + noun; hence, "the Garden of Eden." Sometimes "the" is added to both nouns, creating well-known phrases such as "the fat of the land" or "the house of the Lord," which has found its way onto all Latter-day Saint temples.

This word order is exclusively from Tyndale and is found in many common non-Biblical phrases, including "the law of the land" and the president's "State of the Union" address.

The Book of Mormon follows this proper rendering of Hebrew into English in such descriptions as "the plates of brass" or "the plates of gold," never "the brass plates" or "the golden plates." These later phrases are modern equivalents, but they are not found in the text of the Book of Mormon, thus providing further evidence of its ancient origins. Another Book of Mormon example is "the name of Christ" or "the doctrine of Christ," rather than "Christ's name" or "Christ's doctrine," which sound harsher to the ear. And nobody would dream of exchanging "the sword of Laban" for "Laban's sword." The Doctrine and Covenants also draws upon this construction to produce beautiful sentences. We read of "the beasts of the field," "the fowls of the air," and "the fishes of the sea," which give enchanting music to the creation (D&C 29:24; 59:16).

Tyndale's understanding of the Hebrew superlative produced such musically pleasing descriptions as "the holy of holies" instead of "the holiest place" and "the song of songs" rather than "the best song."[6] He created single words by combining two words he felt best represented the Hebrew, giving us "scapegoat," "shewbread," "taskmaster," and "Passover."

We could add to his list such familiar expressions—some of which came in later books of the Old Testament—as "the Lord's anointed," "am I my brother's keeper," "honor thy father and thy mother," "a land flowing with milk and honey," "an eye for an eye," "male and female created he them," "love the Lord thy God with all thine heart, with all thy soul and with all thy might," "a man after his own heart," "the tree of knowledge of good and evil," "a fool's paradise," and "the breath of life." We hardly give a thought to how perfectly these phrases express the idea behind them and how appropriately the words fit together to make them so unforgettable.

We need only ponder Wycliffe's earlier version of Genesis 1:3— "And God said, Be made light; and made is light"—to realize

Tyndale's uniqueness. Often we do not appreciate why certain biblical phrases have such staying power. In the Garden of Eden, God asked Adam, "Who told thee that thou wast naked?" An examination of the phrase reveals a repeated "th" sound followed by a different vowel sound (*th*ee, *th*at, and *th*ou), and that the repeated "th" is encased between the strong "t" sound in "told" and "wast." The question is rendered perfectly, which we would expect from the being who asked it.

JEHOVAH AND THE URIM AND THUMMIM

Tyndale's most important bestowal on our religious dialect arising out of the Old Testament may be the name *Jehovah*. Judaism did not allow the people to utter the name of deity, so in Hebrew writings the name of God was expressed by the sacred Tetragrammaton, consisting of four consonants: YHWH. This was spoken as Adonai, which we translate as "Lord," but in Exodus 6, Tyndale translated it as Jehovah. At the end of Genesis, he included "A Table Expounding Certain Words." One of those was "Jehovah." Tyndale explains, "Jehovah is God's name, neither is any creature so called. And it is as much to say as one that is of himself, and dependeth on nothing. Moreover as oft as thou seest LORD in great letters, (except there be any error in the printing) it is in Hebrew *Jehovah*, thou that art or he that is."[7]

The King James Version restored to Hebrew a few of Tyndale's translations. For instance, "Urim and Thummim" was translated as "light and perfectness" in Tyndale's 1530 Pentateuch. By way of explanation, he wrote in the margin, "Light and perfectness: In Hebrew it is lights and perfectnesses: and I think that the one were stones that did glister and had light in them and the other clear stones as crystal."[8] That is a rather insightful comment for 1530.

"UNTIL THE WORLD'S END"

The relevancy of Old Testament stories was crucial. Tyndale strived laboriously to make his translation clear, fresh, and understandable, but reading the narratives was not sufficient; they had to be applied. Tyndale offered help. In "A Prologue Showing the Use of the Scripture," he advised:

"If while we fight with ourselves enforcing to walk in the law of God (as they did) we yet fall likewise, that we despair not, but come again to the laws of God and take better hold. . . . Then go to and read the stories of the Bible for thy learning and comfort, and see every thing practiced before thine eyes: for according to those examples shall it go with thee and all men until the world's end. . . . As it went with their kings and rulers, so shall it go with ours. As it was with their common people, so shall it be with ours. As it was with their spiritual officers, so shall it be with ours. As it was with their true prophets, so shall it be with ours until the world's end. . . . All mercy that is shewed there is a promise unto thee, if thou turn to God."[9]

As an example of how to receive "learning and comfort" from the Old Testament, Tyndale detailed the life of Jacob, perhaps the central character in Genesis. The whole passage speaks to mankind's condition and pulses with the empathetic beat of benevolence. Tyndale had no problem equating the Jehovah of the Old Testament with the gentle Jesus of the New Testament. His insight shows an acute understanding of the central theme of the Old Testament and of all scripture. Tyndale was one with humanity, and though alienated by the hateful conduct of many of his nation, he did not lose the native kindness that appears so often in his reflections.

"Mark also the weak infirmities of the man. He loveth one wife more than another, one son more than another. And see how God purgeth him. Esau threateneth him: Laban beguileth him. The beloved wife is long barren: his daughter is ravished: his wife is defiled, and that of his own son. Rachel dieth, Joseph is taken away, yea and as he supposed rent of wild beasts. *And yet how glorious was his end?* Note the weakness of his children, yea and the sin of them, and how God through their own wickedness saved them. *These examples teach us that a man is not at once perfect the first day he beginneth to live well. They that be strong therefore must suffer with the weak."*[10]

The weakness of men was raging in England, a land that at times appeared as harsh as the Old Testament world of the Canaanites or the crushing oppression of Egypt. The heresy hunters were about to light a fire painfully close to Tyndale's heart, and all he could do to ease the loss was press forward with his work. He was right. Men had not changed since the old, cruel times, nor would they change until they applied the words of the Savior, which Tyndale had so painstakingly translated.

NOTES

1. Foxe, *Acts and Monuments,* 5:120.
2. Mozley, *William Tyndale,* 151.
3. Daniell, *Tyndale's Old Testament,* 15.
4. A comparison of Joseph Smith's description of the First Vision in the Pearl of Great Price with Oliver Cowdery's flowery description of the coming of John the Baptist at the end of Joseph Smith–History illustrates the difference.
5. Daniell, *Tyndale's Old Testament,* 7, 8, 10.
6. Bobrick, *Wide As the Waters,* 119.
7. Daniell, *Tyndale's Old Testament,* 82.
8. Ibid., 127.
9. Ibid., 8, 11; spelling standardized.
10. Ibid., 9; emphasis added.

"THAT THE LIGHT GO NOT OUT"

The God of all mercy, and of infinite pity and bottomless compassion, set up this sacrament as a sign on a high hill whence it may be seen on every side, afar and near, to call again them that be fled and run away. And with this sacrament, he (as it were) clucketh to them, as an hen doth for her chickens, to gather them under the wings of his mercy; and hath commanded his sacrament to be had in continual use, to put them in mind of his mercy laid up for them in Christ's blood, and to witness and testify it unto them, and to be the seal thereof. For the sacrament doth much more vehemently print lively the faith, and make it sink down into the heart, than do bare words only: as a man is more sure of that he heareth, seeth, feeleth, smelleth and tasteth, than that he heareth only.

—WILLIAM TYNDALE, *BRIEF DECLARATION OF THE SACRAMENTS*

"SO LEARNED AND EXCELLENT A YOUNG MAN"

Amongst all other chances lamentable, there hath been none a long time which seemed unto me more grievous, than the lamentable death and cruel handling of John Frith, so learned and excellent a young man; who had so profited in all kind of learning and knowledge, that there was scarcely his equal amongst all his companions; and who besides, withal, had such a godliness of life joined with his doctrine, that it was hard to judge in which of them he was more commendable."[1]

Thus Foxe began volume five of his monumental work on the

Christian martyrs. Frith was the dearest friend Tyndale won to his side. Their similarity in intellect and personality drew them like father to son. Frith was a Cambridge man whom Tyndale could have met there or in London during his last year in England. Wherever they met, Tyndale gave birth to Frith's faith, and they loved each other deeply.

A man as eminent as Cardinal Wolsey recognized in Frith great promise and in 1525 included him as a teacher at his new college at Oxford, now called Christ's Church. The reforming spirit soon spread to Oxford in the hearts of its young scholars. A number of them even acquired Tyndale's New Testament when it first crossed the English Channel in 1526. But their conversations were cast under the shadow of heresy, and in 1528 Frith and his friends were imprisoned in a cave under the college where salted fish were stored. The stench and conditions led to the death of three of them, their health having failed after living on salted fish from February to August.

Frith and some of the others were finally released on the condition that they not travel farther than ten miles from Oxford. Some were forced to carry bundles of sticks in procession. Frith, sensing which way the wind was blowing, fled overseas. He married in Holland and worked with Tyndale in Antwerp. In 1531, he made a short spying trip to England, reporting upon his return about conditions there since John Stokesley had been made bishop and Thomas More had been named chancellor. Frith's report on the persecution in England colored Tyndale's refusal to return to his native land when offered safe conduct by Stephen Vaughan, acting in behalf of Thomas Cromwell, the new rising star in the king's court.

Frith returned to England in 1532 and journeyed to Reading to visit the prior of the abbey, a man sympathetic to reform. Was he there to persuade the prior to leave England? Or was the prior an agent in the distribution of Tyndale's publications? Small towns easily recognized strangers, and Frith was arrested as a vagrant. Knowing he was a wanted man, he refused to give his name, but he was not given to fabricating convincing stories, so he was stocked as a vagabond and left to starve. He sent a message to the local schoolmaster, Leonard Cox, desiring to speak with him. Finding Frith well educated and able to quote Homer in Greek, Cox convinced the town leaders to release him, as obviously he was not a vagrant.

Having escaped a close call, Frith went to London, hoping to secretly return to Holland. But the word was out, and reward money was offered to the man who turned him in or caught him. More ordered the ports and roads watched continually. Changing clothes and hiding places almost daily, Frith was finally caught and taken to the Tower of London.

Thomas Cromwell's influence was rising. His sympathy lay with the reformers, especially if they could serve political ends. He secured decent conditions for Frith (he did not have to wear shackles) and kept him, for the time being, out of the hands of Bishop Stokesley. Frith was already in serious trouble for his association with Tyndale and for publications of his own challenging, among other things, the concept of purgatory. Another of his writings cleverly compared the pope's actions and words with those of Christ—the pope coming out on the losing side of the comparison. Yet, for five months Frith stayed in the Tower without suffering any adverse consequences.

Sir Thomas More's Spy

Frith had strong beliefs concerning the sacrament, which he shared with Tyndale. He attended the 1529 meeting between Luther and Huldreich Zwingli in Marburg, where these two giants of the German-Swiss Reformation tried to come together but failed to reach agreement on the nature of the sacrament. Reading Christ's words at the Last Supper, "Take, eat: this is my body. . . . This is my blood" (Matthew 26:26–28) literally instead of figuratively created doctrinal conflicts leading to the death of many during the wars and persecution of the Reformation. From the creeds describing the Godhead to the creation of the Inquisition, literal reading of scripture caused many doctrinal problems. Even burning at the stake was justified by a literal interpretation of Paul's words to the Corinthians: "The fire shall try every man's work of what sort it is" (1 Corinthians 3:13).

While conversing with a close friend, Frith opened his mind on the sacrament, denying the doctrine of transubstantiation. He argued that the Savior's words when instituting the sacrament were meant to be taken figuratively, not literally. "It shall not seem meet or necessary," he stated, "that we should in this place understand Christ's words according to the literal sense, but rather according to the order and phrase of speech."[2]

His arguments were so compelling that a friend visiting him in the Tower asked him to write them down so he could remember them. Frith knew this was dangerous, especially with More and Stokesley on the prowl for further evidence to condemn him. Nevertheless, his nature being one that desired to please, and prevailed upon by his friend, he committed his thoughts to writing.

A London tailor named William Holt, an accomplished spy for the papist party, feigned friendship with Frith's friend, obtained the damaging words, and promptly carried them to More. Eventually three separate copies reached the hands of Sir Thomas, who knew how to efficiently use the underground. Frith explained his predicament in a letter to his friends: "I was loth to take the matter in hand, yet to fulfil his instant intercession, I took upon me to touch this terrible tragedy, and wrote a treatise, which, besides my painful imprisonment, is like to purchase me most cruel death."[3] By this time, More had resigned as chancellor but was as fierce as ever in pursuing heretics. He immediately wrote a treatise, calling attention to Frith's heretical views.

"KEEP A-LOW BY THE GROUND"

Hearing of Frith's imprisonment, Tyndale wrote a letter to him in January 1533, addressing him by the code name "Jacob." Aware of his views on the sacrament, Tyndale warned his friend to be discreet. Unfortunately the advice came too late. The letter, however, further reveals the character of Tyndale and the loving relationship of the two men.

"Dearly beloved brother Jacob, mine heart's desire in our Saviour Jesus is, that you arm yourself with patience, and be cold, sober, wise, and circumspect: that you keep a-low by the ground, avoiding high questions that pass the common capacity." If Frith could avoid controversy, it was advisable to do so. "If you be sure that your part be good, and another hold the contrary, yet if it be a thing that maketh no matter, you will laugh and let it pass, and refer the thing to other men, and stick you stiffly and stubbornly in earnest and necessary things."

They must fight one battle at a time, and the battle for the scriptures was paramount. The battle for the sacrament could be fought later when the principal weapon, the sword of the word, was in English and openly taught throughout the land. Preach repentance and the mercy of Christ, Tyndale encouraged, "and let the wounded consciences drink of the water of him. And then shall your preaching be with power . . . and the Spirit of God shall work with you."[4]

Regarding the sacrament, Tyndale offered this late advice: "Of the presence of Christ's body in the sacrament, meddle as little as you can." One of the reasons for this advice was the lack of unity among the reformers on the subject. "You perceive my mind," Tyndale continued, "howbeit, if God show you otherwise, it is free for you to do as he moveth you." But in all occasions, Frith was to "thrust in, that the Scripture may be in the mother tongue. . . . Then stand fast, and commit yourself to God, and be not overcome of men's persuasions."

Frith was as close to a son as Tyndale would ever have. In tones denoting a father's love, he continued:

"Brother Jacob, beloved in my heart! there liveth not in whom I have so good hope and trust, and in whom my heart rejoiceth, and my soul comforteth herself, as in you. . . . Finally, if there were in me any gift that could help at hand, and aid you if need required, I promise you I would not be far off, and commit the end to God. My soul is not faint, though my body the weary. But God hath made me evil-favored in this world, and without grace in the sight of men, speechless and rude, dull and slow-witted: your part shall be to supply what lacketh in me; remembering that as lowliness of heart shall make you high with God, even so meekness of words shall make you sink into the hearts of men."[5]

THE DISCIPLE DEFENDS THE MASTER

The letter did come in time to help Frith reply to More's condemnation of his belief concerning the sacrament. In that reply, Frith defended his mentor and spiritual father:

"Tyndale, I trust, liveth, well content with such a poor apostle's life, as God gave his son Christ and his faithful ministers in this world, which is not sure of so many mites as ye [More] be yearly of pounds, although I am sure that for his learning and judgment in scripture he were more worthy to be promoted than all the bishops in England. . . . And as for his behavior, [it] is such that I am sure no man can reprove him of any sin."[6]

Tyndale was not becoming rich on his smuggled scriptures. They were designed to be affordable to the average laboring man. Frith quoted part of Tyndale's letter in which Tyndale stated the sincerity of his translating efforts: "I call God to record against the day we shall appear before our Lord Jesus, to give a reckoning of our doings, that I never altered one syllable of God's word against my conscience, nor would this day, if all that is in the earth, whether it be pleasure, honour, or riches, might be given me."[7] Luther would not even go that far, instead tweaking a verse here and there to lean it more favorably to his views.

Frith embodied the same zeal for the Bible in English that burned in Tyndale's heart. Master and pupil were one in the great cause entrusted to them by God. Frith made an offer in behalf of them both that shows their sincerity, an offer that Tyndale had made earlier:

"The word of God boileth in my body like a fervent fire, and will needs have an issue, and break out when occasion is given. But this hath been offered, is offered, and shall be offered:—grant that the word of God, I mean the text of scripture, may go abroad in our English tongue, as other nations have it in their tongues, and my brother William Tyndale and I have done, and will promise you to write no more. If you will not grant this condition, then will we be doing while we have breath . . . and so at the least save some."[8]

Bootleg Writings from the Tower

Frith's writings from prison were come by dearly. He could not freely write refutations to More but did so secretly with the help of friends who visited him in the Tower and a jailor willing to look the other way. According to early documents, the under-keeper of the Tower, a man named Phillips, sometimes opened the door at night and let Frith visit friends. One of those friends was John Petit, a grocer who had overseas connections to the reformers and who had spent time in the Tower as the unwilling guest of Sir Thomas. Petit was lucky he was not burned. A search party led by Sir Thomas himself failed to notice a copy of Tyndale's New Testament lying openly under a desk in Petit's house. Petit accepted the oversight as evidence the Lord was watching over the efforts of the "Bible men." More was loathe to release him but in time had no choice. Now Petit was dangerously aiding Frith.

Other guards of the Tower's prisoners were not so lax in their duty, and Frith had to be careful. He described his conditions in an apology for the "rudeness and imperfection" of his defense of the sacrament as a memorial (as opposed to its transubstantiation) in one of the treatises he smuggled out of prison:

"I am in a manner as a man bound to a post, and cannot so well bestow me in my play, as if I were at liberty; for I may not have such books as are necessary for me, neither yet pen, ink, nor paper, but only secretly, so that I am in continual fear both of the lieutenant and of my keeper, lest they should espy any such thing by me; and therefore it is little marvel though the work be imperfect, for whensoever

I hear the keys ring at the door, straight all must be conveyed out of the way; and then if any notable thing had been in my mind, it was clean lost."[9]

THE CHANCE TO ESCAPE

Frith's case came to a head with the preaching of a scathing sermon in front of Henry VIII. Little wonder heresy was circulating, the fiery cleric suggested, for even as he spoke there was one in the Tower still living and uncondemned who preached against the sacrament. Sir Thomas More wrote a private letter to Henry, reminding him of his title, Defender of the Faith, and that it had been won while defending the seven sacraments of the church. Though he had resigned as chancellor, Sir Thomas still fought to bring Tyndale's friends to the stake. To More, Frith's beliefs regarding the sacrament "should cost him the best blood in his body." More was certain "Christ will kindle a fire of faggots for him and . . . send his soul for ever into the fires of hell."[10] Thus pressed, Henry gave instructions that Frith be brought to trial.

Frith was a beloved young man with great promise. The reform-minded Thomas Cromwell and Archbishop Thomas Cranmer were now in positions of influence; perhaps an escape could be arranged. During Frith's transport to Croydon for his inquisition, his carefully selected porters, having failed to convince him to recant, suggested he slip away into the woods while they directed pursuers to search in the opposite direction. To this suggestion, Frith responded, "If you should both leave me here, and go to Croydon declaring to the bishops that you had lost Frith, I would surely follow after as fast as I might, and bring them news that I had found and brought Frith again." When asked why he was willing to choose such extreme danger when earlier he had tried desperately to escape to his wife and Tyndale across the Channel, Frith replied that he had need now to be bold, testifying of his faith and remaining true to the cause of God.[11] At length he was brought before Bishop Stokesley, condemned as a heretic, and delivered over for burning.

The burning of John Frith and Andrew Hewet.

A young apprentice tailor named Andrew Hewet joined Frith in his execution. Hewet had been betrayed by the same sly William Holt, who had turned in Frith. Hewet's reply to Bishop Stokesley showed the fierce loyalty Tyndale and Frith had created in their fellowmen. When asked about his faith in the sacrament, Hewet answered as he believed: "Even as John Frith doth." But Frith, Stokesley countered, "is a heretic, and already judged to be burned; and except thou revoke thine opinion, thou shalt be burned also with him." Hewet replied, "Truly, I am content therewithal."[12]

Tied back-to-back, they were burned as "obstinate, impenitent, and incorrigible heretics" on July 4, 1533.[13] One of them received the benefit of a blowing wind, the other greater suffering. Frith was not the favored one, but "God giving him strength . . . he seemed rather to rejoice for his fellow, than to be careful for himself."[14]

"A LIGHT FED WITH THE BLOOD OF FAITH"

Frith had been strengthened by his spiritual father, who prayed fervently for him in Antwerp while waiting, almost without hope, for news of the young man who had become a son to him. Tyndale wrote him a final letter when all hope seemed lost. Whether Frith received it in time is unknown, but the spirit of the letter breathes with the soul of its author and his knowledge that he would not see the young man again until the Judgment called the righteous from the grave. This time Tyndale dropped the code name and addressed Frith directly as his "Dearly beloved brother John," writing:

"However the matter be, commit yourself wholly and only unto your most loving Father, and most kind Lord. Fear not men that threat, nor trust men that speak fair; but trust him that is true of promise, and able to make his word good. Your cause is Christ's gospel, a light that must be fed with the blood of faith. The lamp must be dressed and snuffed daily, and that oil poured in every evening and morning, that the light go not out. Though we be sinners, yet is the cause right. . . . Rejoice and be glad, for great is your reward in heaven. For we suffer with him, that we may also be glorified with him. . . .

"Dearly beloved! be of good courage, and comfort your soul with the hope of this high reward, and bear the image of Christ in your mortal body, that it may, at his coming, be made like to his, immortal; and follow the example of all your other dear brethren, who choose to suffer in hope of a better resurrection. . . . If you give yourself, cast yourself, yield yourself, commit yourself, wholly and only to your living Father; then shall his power be in you, and make you strong; and that so strong, that you shall feel no pain. . . . He shall set out his truth by you wonderfully, and work for you above all that your heart can imagine. . . .

"There falleth not a hair, till his hour be come; and when his hour is come, necessity carrieth us hence, though we be not willing. But if we be willing, then have we a reward and thank. . . . If the pain be above your strength, remember, 'whatsoever ye shall ask in my name, I will give it you.' And pray to your Father in that name, and he shall ease your pain, or shorten it. . . .

"Two have suffered in Antwerp . . . four at Ryselles [Lille] in Flanders, and at Luke [Liege] hath there one at the least suffered; and all the same day. At Rouen in France they persecute, and at Paris are five doctors taken for the gospel. See, you are not alone; be cheerful. . . . The Lord be yet again with you with all his plenteousness, and fill you that you flow over. Amen.

"Sir, your wife is well content with the will of God, and would not, for her sake, have the glory of God hindered."[15]

The letter is a treasure in its dignity and tenderness. Tyndale knew his friend, and his confidence was not misplaced. Frith never wavered. As Mozley wrote, "The disciple was worthy of the master. There was no fear of him recanting; he had learnt his lesson too well."[16] The last poignant remark of Tyndale's letter reveals that the wives of men like Frith were equal in conviction and remained true in the face of their own intense suffering. We also learn from the letter that life in Antwerp was becoming more dangerous, two men being martyred even in the tolerant atmosphere of the city. Tyndale was really never safe anywhere he traveled.

BATTLES JOSEPH SMITH WOULD NOT NEED TO FIGHT

The Lord accomplished several purposes through the Reformation, which was without question a necessary step preceding the Restoration. The Reformation created Christian diversity, thus breaking the power of one dominant creed and paving the way for eventual tolerance. It also fought many battles for the Prophet Joseph Smith. He did not need to fight the battle of infant baptism; the Anabaptists fought and died to challenge that doctrine. He did not need to fight the battle of a lay priesthood; Luther and Calvin accomplished that. Frith died for the sacrament, which Christ gave as a simple ceremony designed to remind God's children of his atoning sacrifice. By 1820, the idea that the sacrament was a memorial, not the literal body and blood of Christ changed by the priest, was a well-established Protestant tenet.

Tyndale fought the battle of the ploughboy with a Bible in his hand. Joseph Smith would still have to fight, but God spared him a large number of battles that cost the lives of many hundreds of devoted, promising, faith-filled people and the tears of those who loved them.

NOTES

1. Foxe, *Acts and Monuments,* 5:2.
2. Ibid., 5:6.
3. Mozley, *William Tyndale,* 246–47.
4. Foxe, *Acts and Monuments,* 5:133.
5. Ibid., 5:134.
6. Mozley, *William Tyndale,* 251–52.
7. Foxe, *Acts and Monuments,* 5:134.
8. Mozley, *William Tyndale,* 252.

9. Ibid., 254–55.

10. Ackroyd, *Life of Thomas More,* 333.

11. Mozley, *William Tyndale,* 256.

12. Foxe, *Acts and Monuments,* 5:17–18.

13. Ibid., 5:16.

14. Ibid., 5:15.

15. Ibid., 5:131–32.

16. Mozley, *William Tyndale,* 260.

AN UNSAFE
SAFE CONDUCT

Mark this then: to see inwardly that the law of God is so spiritual, that no flesh can fulfill it; and then to mourn and sorrow,
and to desire, yea, to hunger and thirst after strength to do the
will of God from the ground of the heart, and (notwithstanding
all the subtilty of the devil, weakness and feebleness of the flesh,
and wondering of the world) to cleave yet to the promises of God,
and to believe that for Christ's blood sake thou art received to the
inheritance of eternal life, is a wonderful thing, and a thing that
the world knoweth not of; but whosoever feeleth that, though he
fall a thousand times in a day, doth yet rise again a thousand
times, and is sure that the mercy of God is upon him.

—WILLIAM TYNDALE, *THE PARABLE OF THE WICKED MAMMON*

THE KING'S GREAT MATTER

The lives of Tyndale, More, Wolsey, and indeed of all
Britons and many Europeans were deeply affected by what
became known as "The King's Great Matter." Henry's
father, Henry VII, came to the throne at the conclusion of a mur-
derous inter-family rivalry for control of England called the Wars of
the Roses. Henry VIII had no desire to see the country plunged into
civil war again, and he believed a male heir was necessary to avoid
it. Anne Boleyn's entrance into the court as a maid of honor only
intensified Henry's mood, especially because she was unwilling to
yield to him until she was queen of England.

Cardinal Wolsey fell from power because he failed to secure

from Pope Clement VII the king's divorce. Even if he wanted to grant it, the pope was hamstrung. He was in the control of Charles V, the holy Roman emperor who just happened to be the nephew of Catherine of Aragon, Henry's first wife.

Tyndale felt he needed to enter the fray. It was an opportunity to challenge the influence of the church, particularly illustrated by Cardinal Wolsey, whom Tyndale nicknamed "Wolfsee" because he preyed on the lambs of England. Tyndale wrote a small treatise called *The Practice of Prelates*. It had an interesting subtitle: "Whether the King's grace may be separated from his queen because she was his brother's wife."[1] It was printed in Antwerp by Hoochstraten, though Marburg appeared on the publication as its printing site.

Tyndale was not afraid to wade into dangerous waters. Though he could have bettered his situation enormously by giving reasons justifying Henry's marriage to Anne Boleyn, he did just the opposite, arguing for Queen Catherine with the force of scripture. His innocence shows through again. In the world of politics, he could not be ingratiating. He was born to tell the truth, not curry favor, and political correctness was an idea Tyndale would have disdained as unchristian.

Tyndale's arguments were bound to alienate the one man who could grant his deepest desire. Henry was offended by the treatise, and in typical kingly manner he raged against the audacity of the exiled heretic. *The Practice of Prelates* is Tyndale's least desirable work. We would gladly exchange it for an equal number of translated pages of the prophets or the Psalms. But suddenly the king's rage subsided, and overtures were made to Tyndale to return to England, apparently at the king's invitation.

Charles V's ambassador, Eustace Chapuys, better described as an imperial spy, reported that Henry, "afraid lest the priest Tyndale shall write more boldly against him, and hoping to persuade him to retract what he has already written, has invited him back to England, and offered him several good appointments and a seat in his council."[2] That was quite a change if the report, which Chapuys assured his government was from the most trustworthy of sources, was correct. The explanation behind this mysterious change of attitude was found in a new power at court, Thomas Cromwell.

Thomas Cromwell—Reformer's Friend

Cromwell was a brewer's son and a one-time mercenary who rose through his studies of the law, first to a place by the side of Wolsey, then to the side of the king. He orchestrated the divesting of the Catholic Church of its power in England. Pushing act after act through Parliament, Cromwell, with the help of Bishop Thomas Cranmer, overawed the clergy, abolished payments to Rome, nullified Henry's marriage to Catherine, and married Henry to Anne. Excommunicated by the pope, Cromwell, Cranmer, and Henry had Parliament pass the Act of Supremacy, making the Church of England a separate institution with Henry as its head. This rapid succession of events took place between 1532 and 1534 and illustrates the enormous influence Cromwell wielded during those years.

Sir Thomas More once counseled Cromwell regarding his service to the king, saying, "Ever tell him what he ought to do but never what he is able to do. . . . For if a lion knew his own strength, hard were it for any man to rule him."[3] Cromwell taught the royal lion that he had teeth!

Would Cromwell's sway be sufficient to end Tyndale's self-imposed exile and allow his great vision of an English Bible to be fulfilled? Cromwell leaned toward the reformers and set about reconciliation with Tyndale. Apparently, he suggested to Henry that a pen as mighty as Tyndale's might be a good ally to have in his corner. After all, Tyndale had written strongly against clerical abuses and suggested in *The Obedience of a Christian Man,* which the king's beloved Anne had shared with him, the proper role of spiritual and secular powers.

Henry's agent to bring all this about was a man named Stephen Vaughan. Vaughan was a merchant adventurer with connections in Antwerp. The merchants plying their trade between England and the Netherlands had strong reforming sympathies and supported Tyndale with both money and smuggling avenues.

SAFE CONDUCT

While John Frith was stealing across the English Channel and through the English countryside, Vaughan was looking for Tyndale back on the Continent. Cromwell had commissioned Vaughan to find Tyndale and learn his feelings on returning to England under a safe conduct. Vaughan had a tough assignment. Safe conducts were reliably unsafe. The Prague reformer Jan Hus was burned in Constance in 1415 under the promise of safe conduct. No promise need be kept with a heretic, the church council reasoned.

During Vaughan's mission, Robert Barnes was granted safe conduct to return to England in 1531. He had earlier carried a bundle of sticks at St. Paul's Cross under the watchful eye of Wolsey in 1526. He recanted and fled to the Continent, but he was granted safe conduct in England for six weeks.[4] He had written a strong diatribe against the pope, and Henry was interested in such learned men for his own political purposes. Sir Thomas More, eager to condemn such an obvious heretic, wrote, "Yet hath he so demeaned himself, since his coming hither, that he had clearly broken and forfeited his safe conduct, and lawfully might be burned." But Barnes was allowed to leave, and More bitterly commented, "Let him go this once, for God shall find his time full well."[5] More was never known to show an ounce of mercy to a heretic, and the promise of a king mattered little if an opponent of the church could be eliminated.

Tyndale, though gentle and trusting in nature, was becoming streetwise, especially as news of the arrest of Thomas Bilney and Thomas Hitton filtered across the Channel. Tyndale's brother John was arrested in 1530 "for sending five marks to his brother William Tyndale beyond the sea, and for receiving and keeping with him certain letters from his brother."[6] For these "crimes," Bishop Stokesley and More required John and others accused of aiding the work overseas to do penance.[7] They had to ride a horse with their faces toward the tail "and to have papers upon their heads, and . . . upon their gowns and cloaks to be tacked or pinned thick with the said New Testaments and other books." After parading through the market place, they threw the offending books into a fire and paid a fine.[8]

Another friend, William Tracy, had written a will that was circulating in England. In it he refused to set aside money for prayers on behalf of his soul because he relied on the mercy of Christ alone and needed no other mediator. This was a dangerous attack on a lucrative source of income and could not be ignored. The ecclesiastics were outraged and threatened to exhume Tracy's body and burn it for heresy. A year later, they carried out their threat.

A Suspected Trap

In this atmosphere, Vaughan began his search. We know a great deal of Vaughan's contacts with Tyndale because his letters have survived. He wrote to the king in January 1531 from the Netherlands. He had searched far and wide, offering the promised safe conduct but without success. "My endeavors have been repeatedly brought to nought, whereat I am right sorry," he begins. "I have written three sundry letters unto William Tyndale, and the same sent . . . to Frankfurt, Hamburg and Marburg."[9]

Vaughan guessed the reason for his difficulty. "The bruit [noise] and fame of such things as, since my writing to him, hath chanced within your realm, has led him not only to refuse, but to suspect a trap to bring him into peril."[10] The network of Tyndale's friends, however, had found him, showed him one of Vaughan's letters, and elicited an answer from him, which was delivered to Vaughan. The letter, Vaughan wrote, mentions a book Tyndale and Frith were working on as a response to Sir Thomas More's attacks.[11]

Vaughan added a note for Cromwell's eyes. "It is unlikely to get Tyndale into England, when he daily heareth so many things from thence which feareth him. . . . The man is of a greater knowledge than the king's highness doth take him for; which well appeareth by his works. Would God he were in England!"[12]

Even from afar, Tyndale impressed others with his learning and his Christian soul. His contacts were extensive, organized to the point that, if we accept Vaughan's word at face value, he received news daily. Still trying to arrange an interview in March, Vaughan wrote, "I can little or nothing profit with him by my letters, for so much as the man hath me greatly suspected."[13]

"DO YOU NOT KNOW ME?"

By April 1531, the unexpected happened when Vaughan at last found Tyndale. He described the encounter in great detail. His description is part of a precious document that gives one of the few personal portrayals of Tyndale while he was hiding in Europe:

"He sent a certain person to seek me, whom he had advised to say that a certain friend of mine, unknown to the messenger, was very desirous to speak with me; praying me to take pains to go unto him, to such place as he should bring me. Then I to the messenger, 'What is your friend, and where is he?' 'His name I know not,' said he; 'but if it be your pleasure to go where he is, I will be glad thither to bring you.' Thus, doubtful what this matter meant, I concluded to go with him, and followed him till he brought me without the gates of Antwerp, into a field lying nigh unto the same; where was abiding me this said Tyndale.

"At our meeting, 'Do you not know me?' said this Tyndale. 'I do not well remember you,' said I to him. 'My name,' said he, 'is Tyndale.' 'But Tyndale!' said I, 'fortunate be our meeting.' Then Tyndale, 'Sir, I have been exceeding desirous to speak with you.' 'And I with you; what is your mind?' 'Sir,' said he, 'I am informed that the king's grace taketh great displeasure with me for putting forth of certain books, which I lately made in these parts; but . . . I did but warn his grace of the subtle demeanour of the clergy of his realm towards his person . . . in which doing I showed and declared the heart of a true subject, which sought the safeguard of his royal person and weal [well-being] of his commons. . . . If for my pains therein taken, if for my poverty, if for mine exile out of my natural country, and bitter absence from my friends, if for my hunger, my thirst, my cold, the great danger wherewith I am everywhere encompassed, and finally if for innumerable other hard and sharp fightings which I endure, not yet feeling their asperity [bitterness] by reason I hoped with my labours to do honour to God, true service to my prince, and pleasure to his commons; how is it that his grace, this considering, may either by himself think, or by the persuasions of others be brought to think, that in this doing I should not show a pure mind, a true and incorrupt zeal and affection to his grace? . . . Doth this deserve hatred?

"'Again, may his grace, being a Christian prince, be so unkind to God, which hath commanded his word to be spread throughout the world, to give more faith to the wicked persuasions of men, which, presuming above God's wisdom, and contrary to that which Christ expressly commandeth in his testament, dare say that it is not lawful for the people to have the same in a tongue that they understand, because the purity thereof should open men's eyes to see their wickedness? Is there more danger in the king's subjects than in the subjects of all other princes, which in every of their tongues have the same, under privilege of their sovereigns? As I now am, very death were more pleasant to me than life.'"[14]

It is clear Tyndale thought the king was a key to bringing the Lord's word to the English "commons." It is also clear that he did not know how to court favor from a powerful monarch and was unsure of the king's motives. He was guided by one single driving purpose, one so logical that everyone should have seen its virtue. However, Sir Thomas More had earlier persuaded the king to declare that "divulging [the whole of Scripture] at this time in English to the people, should rather be to their farther confusion and destruction, than to the edification of their souls."[15]

Into the Shadow of Twilight

Vaughan's letter provides a glimpse of the life Tyndale lived during his years of exile. Filled with danger, poverty, and physical hardship, his life echoed Paul's description of his own labors (2 Corinthians 11:23–33). Yet he had not lost the candid, innocent purity of character demonstrated earlier. He found it difficult to understand why he was viewed as an enemy to the realm rather than as a benefactor. Every reasonable man should see the need for the scriptures in English and appreciate the sacrifices Tyndale was enduring to make them available. "Doth this deserve hatred?" has a poignant ring to it. Tyndale, though a loyal subject of his majesty, had a higher duty to God and the work God had assigned to him. Vaughan's letter continues, showing the constant vigilance Tyndale was forced to keep:

"I assayed him with gentle persuasions, to know whether he would come into England; ascertaining [assuring] him that means should be made, if he thereto were minded, without his peril or danger, that he might so do; and that what surety he would devise for the same purpose. . . . But to this he answered, that he neither would nor durst come into England, albeit your grace would promise him never so much the surety; fearing lest, as he hath before written, your promise made should shortly be broken, by the persuasion of the clergy, which would affirm that promises made with heretics ought not to be kept. . . .

"After these words, he then, being something fearful of me, lest I would have pursued him, and drawing also towards night, he took his leave of me, and departed from the town, and I toward the town. . . . Howbeit I suppose he afterward returned to the town by another way; for there is no likelihood that he should lodge without the town."[16]

THE KING'S RAGE

In his letter to the king, Vaughan continued, "To declare to your majesty what, in my poor judgment, I think of the man, I ascertain your grace, I have not communed with a man . . . "[17] Here the letter is torn, and the last portion of it lost to history. We can judge from other comments made by Vaughan that he was about to praise

Tyndale, for Cromwell later warned him that his own future was in jeopardy if he defended Tyndale too enthusiastically. As circumstances later proved, Sir Thomas More immediately began to inquire into the leanings and loyalties of Vaughan in such a manner as to terrify him. There is no doubt that Vaughan was deeply impressed by and empathetic toward the man he met in the shadows of Antwerp's walls.

As can be expected, Henry did not respond favorably to Vaughan's letter. Tyndale was supposed to return penitently, suing for clemency, hat in hand, kneeling in contrition for his offending actions and words. Instead, he challenged the validity of the promised safe conduct and questioned the king's wisdom in forbidding the translations to circulate freely. He doubted the word of a king who he felt operated under the counsel of his enemies—the clergy and Sir Thomas More. Cromwell wrote to Vaughan, expressing the king's displeasure in rather strong language:

"The king's highness . . . hath commanded me to advertise you, that ye should desist and leave any further to persuade or attempt the said Tyndale to come into this realm; alleging that he, perceiving the malicious, perverse, uncharitable, and indurate mind of the said Tyndale, is in manner without hope of reconciliation in him, and is very joyous to have his realm destitute of such a person, than that he should return into the same, there to manifest his errors and seditious opinions, which, being out of the realm, by his most uncharitable, venomous and pestilent books, crafty and false persuasions he hath partly done already. For his highness right prudently considereth, if he were present, by all likelihood he would shortly (which God defend) do as much as in him were to infect and corrupt the whole realm, to the great inquietation and hurt of the commonwealth of the same."[18]

These are harsh words for a man whose intentions were so selfless. But in all likelihood, they are the sentiments of More and Stokesley rather than the true feelings of Henry VIII. How much of Tyndale's actual writing the king had read is unknown. We know

Anne Boleyn showed him passages in *The Obedience of a Christian Man,* but he left much to his advisers. Cromwell, still hopeful of enlisting Tyndale in the king's cause, added his own postscript to Vaughan, encouraging him to continue to persuade Tyndale.

"WATER STOOD IN HIS EYES"

Vaughan soon had another interview with Tyndale, the details of which he passed on to Cromwell and the king:

"I have again been in hand to persuade Tyndale . . . [and] I showed him a clause contained in Master Cromwell's letter, containing these words following:—if it were possible, by good and wholesome exhortations, to reconcile and convert the said Tyndale . . . and take away the opinions and fantasies sorely rooted in him, I doubt not but the king's highness would be much joyous of his conversion and amendment; and so being converted, if then he would return into this realm, undoubtedly the king's royal majesty is so inclined to mercy, pity, and compassion that he refuseth none which he seeth to submit themselves to the obedience and good order of the world."[19]

Here was Tyndale's opportunity. He could come home to a merciful king, end his exile, and enjoy family and country if he would amend his ways. Tyndale was deeply moved by Cromwell's letter.

"I perceived the man to be exceedingly altered," Vaughan continued, "in such wise that water stood in his eyes, and answered, 'What gracious words are these! I assure you,' said he, 'if it would stand with the king's most gracious pleasure to grant only a bare text of the scripture to be put forth among his people . . . be it of the translation of what person soever shall please his majesty, I shall immediately make faithful promise never to write more, nor abide two days in these parts after the same; but immediately to repair into his realm, and there most humbly submit myself at the feet of his royal majesty, offering my body to suffer what pain or torture, yea, what death his grace will, so this be obtained."[20]

Here is the heart and soul of the man. From the moment his

resolve was formed in Little Sodbury, he had stayed true to the fire in his bones. He sought no credit. He wanted no fame. He cared not for wealth. He was not afraid of pain or death. The king could decide punishment. He only wanted his countrymen to know the sweetness of the Testaments and to hear the voice of Jesus in their own language. It did not matter who did the translating. The bare text without any comments was enough. He would silence his pen forever. However, if permission was not granted, Tyndale would continue the hardships he was bearing. No man, no argument, no threat, no promise could sway him. A flame lit by God marked his path, and he had the courage to walk it. Tyndale's last words to Vaughan ring with his commitment.

"And Passeth Any Man's Power to Stop Them"

"And till that time, I will abide the asperity of all chances, whatsoever shall come, and endure my life in as many pains as it is able to bear and suffer. And as concerning my reconciliation, his grace may be assured that, whatsoever I have said or written in all my life against the honour of God's word, and so proved, the same shall I before his majesty and all the world utterly renounce and forsake, and with most humble and meek mind embrace the truth, abhorring all error, sooner at the most gracious and benign request of his royal majesty, of whose wisdom, prudence, and learning I hear so great praise and commendation, than of any other creature living. But if those things which I have written be true, and stand with God's word, why should his majesty, having so excellent gift of knowledge in the scriptures, move me to do anything against my conscience?"[21]

So many times we hear the voice of Joseph Smith in the convictions of Tyndale. The world also tried to make Joseph deny what he knew to be true, but having the same steadfast courage as Tyndale, he wrote, "I was led to say in my heart: Why persecute me for telling the truth? . . . Who am I that I can withstand God, or why does the world think to make me deny what I have actually seen?" (Joseph Smith–History 1:25).

Vaughan had one final meeting with Tyndale. We do not know what passed between the two men. Yet Vaughan expressed the wish that the king read Tyndale's words rather than have them evaluated by others. If Henry would peruse them himself, he would see that Tyndale was not writing to "eloquent men." His style was "simple . . . nothing seeking any vain praise and commendation. If the king's royal pleasure had been to have looked thereupon, he should then have better judged it than upon the sight of another man." Vaughan then added, "The prophets Esay [Isaiah] . . . and Jonas . . . are put forth in the English tongue, and passeth any man's power to stop them from coming forth."[22]

Tyndale continued working while conversing with Vaughan. His translation of Jonah then circulating in England was proof that he intended to press forward. Sadly, he felt a need to answer the man who was reading his publications and turning the king against them. Sir Thomas More had thrown down the gauntlet. Tyndale paused in his work with the Old Testament to pick it up. The duel between the two great men was now fully engaged.

NOTES

1. When Henry came to the throne in 1509, he married his brother's widow, Catherine. She bore him five children, but only one, a daughter, lived to adulthood.
2. Daniell, *William Tyndale*, 210.
3. Ackroyd, *Life of Thomas More*, 196.
4. Ibid., 305–6.
5. Daniell, *William Tyndale*, 211.
6. Foxe, *Acts and Monuments*, 5:29.
7. The Star Chamber pronounced judgment.
8. Mozley, *William Tyndale*, 171.
9. Ibid., 187; spelling standardized.
10. Ibid.

11. A legendary encounter between Tyndale and More is discussed in the next chapter.
12. Mozley, *William Tyndale*, 188–89.
13. Ibid., 192.
14. Ibid., 193–94.
15. Bobrick, *Wide As the Waters*, 130.
16. Mozley, *William Tyndale*, 194–95.
17. Ibid., 195.
18. Ibid., 196–97.
19. Ibid., 198.
20. Ibid., 198–99.
21. Ibid., 199.
22. Ibid., 200.

THE GREAT DUEL

𝔚ho taught the eagles to spy out their prey? Even so the children of God spy out their ffather; and Christ's elect spy out their Lord, and trace out the paths of his feet and follow; yea, though he go upon the plain and liquid water, which will receive no step, and yet there they find out his foot: his elect know him, but the world knoweth him not.

—WILLIAM TYNDALE, *AN ANSWER UNTO SIR THOMAS MORE'S DIALOGUE*

THE MAN FOR ALL SEASONS

Sir Thomas More's ward and later daughter-in-law, Anne Cresacre, once asked him for a pearl necklace. He later presented her with a box, saying, "I have not forgotten." She opened the box, but instead of the expected pearls she found a string of garden peas. This was More's method of teaching Anne the dangers of vanity. She wept for grief, but he contented himself with the knowledge that she was the better for the lesson.[1]

This story is not an example of his harshness, for he disciplined his children by beating them with peacock feathers. Rather, it shows his desire to instill character. He wanted his children to find their studies pleasant, so he put Latin and Greek letters on the archery range so they could memorize them while shooting at them.

More married Jane Colt, the eldest daughter of "one Master Colt," though "his mind most served him to the second daughter, for that he thought her the fairest and best favored, yet when he considered that it would be both great grief and some shame also to the eldest to see her younger sister in marriage preferred before her, he then . . . framed his fancy towards her."[2] He married Jane when she was sixteen, educating her in all the cultural learning of the day—as he did their daughters—at a time when educating women was rare.

Refined and well-dressed, More wore an irritating hair shirt next to his skin from his early manhood to tame the temptations of the flesh. Not content, he also scourged himself with knotted cords, allowing only his daughter Margaret, who washed his shirt, to know. He was the greatest English humanist of his age, perhaps the greatest of all Europe. He was brilliant, witty, hospitable, and absolutely devoted to his family and his Catholic faith. He had a fine sense of justice (in all matters except heresy), refusing the common practice of receiving bribes. He once handed out a judgment against his own son-in-law when pressured for a favorable verdict. He was deeply generous, caring for the poor at his manor in Chelsea, even building a separate house for them. He often remitted his legal fees.

Whenever a woman in the parish was in labor, he knelt and prayed until the child was delivered. This gentle concern may have resulted from the loss of his wife, who died at twenty-two in childbirth. It was said that he could always bring a smile or laughter, so fine was his sense of humor. Erasmus hailed him as a close friend, calling him *omnium horarum*—"a man for all seasons." Robert Whittinton drew upon Erasmus when he wrote, "More is a man of an angel's wit and singular learning; I know not his fellow. For where is the man of that gentleness, lowliness, and affability? And as time requireth a man of marvelous mirth and pastimes; and sometimes of as sad gravity: a man for all seasons."[3]

In More, the dark old world of misplaced faith mingled with the new world of learning and enlightenment. In the clash of belief and reason, in the crisis of his life played out against the larger crisis of his nation, he clung to the old dogmas and fears. An otherwise magnificent mind remained in captivity, burdened by the weight of apostasy's yoke of iron.

Authority or Anarchy

Like Tyndale, More was exceptionally intelligent as a child and schooled in the classics. Tyndale turned with fervor to scripture; More was equally zealous for the traditions of the Roman Catholic Church. Both were Oxford men. More was not ignorant of the abuses of the clergy and approved of Erasmus' satirical commentaries on the church. But when Luther launched the Reformation, few rose to defend the old order as vehemently as Sir Thomas More.

He was a lawyer and a believer in authority. Even as chancellor of England, he knelt before his father when he saw him in the courts and asked for his blessing. The greatest authority on earth was the Catholic Church. A challenge to that body was an invitation to anarchy, a word that More brought into English from the Greek. Tyndale was a man of the Bible, whose authority predated the church. His worship was that of private prayer. His faith centered in Christ rather than in the ritual of the mass. The confrontation between More and Tyndale at a great crossroad of history was symbolic and inevitable.

Tyndale stated that the apostasy occurred because when "they that had the plough by the tail *looked back,* the plough went awry; faith waxed feeble and fainty; love waxed cold; the scripture waxed dark; Christ was no more seen."[4] Tyndale turned with the world to a new sunrise, influencing millions of future generations yet remaining almost unknown. More continued looking backward into the apostate night, touching future generations only mildly yet being honored as a saint for remaining true to his faith. Such are the ironies of life.

Sir Thomas rose quickly in the elite circle of Henry VIII's court, serving as speaker of the House of Commons in 1523. When Henry wrote his treatise against Luther, for which he received the title "Defender of the Faith," More was there to aid him. Henry's treatise referred to Tyndale as a "lewd" person who translated the Bible into English with the purpose of abusing the minds and devotions of the people. More, an able writer, produced *Utopia,* which is still studied as a classic of English literature. When pressed, he turned his talents to the defense of his faith, doing so with fervor and ferocity.

WHERE THE TWISTING SERPENTS LURK

In 1523, More wrote his *Responsio ad Lutherum,* a vitriolic work attacking Luther with a mountain of vulgar language. More did not hesitate using gutter expressions of the lowest levels of the street, though he did so in grammatically correct Latin. He wrote under a pen name, but everyone knew the author who had taken on the German monk. The language of the day was rough, but even for the times, More was scalding. After all, Luther stood against all More believed was the foundation of ordered life. That order had treated More well, he was loyal to it, and he feared the collapse of society if the reformers were not silenced. If that required filth and fire, then God approved.

When Tyndale smuggled his Bibles and treatises into England, the war against reform shifted to the home front in a perilous manner. Bishop Cuthbert Tunstall gave Sir Thomas More license to read the heretical books that he might refute them. "I am sending you their mad incantations," Tunstall wrote, "in our tongue . . . [that] you will understand more easily in what hiding places these twisting serpents lurk."[5] More went eagerly to the task, and in June 1529 he published his *Dialogue Concerning Heresies.* Because his opponent published in English, More did also. He struck the initial blow against Tyndale, one Tyndale probably never saw coming. He must have been frustrated to leave the task so near his heart to respond to this new and vocal enemy.

SEWING UP HOLES IN A NET

More had to crush Tyndale, for if Tyndale prevailed, all More loved would vanish. "If Tyndale's testament be taken up," he argued, "then shall false heresies be preached, then shall the sacraments be set at naught, then shall fasting and prayer be neglected, then shall holy saints be blasphemed, then shall Almighty God be displeased, then shall he withdraw his grace and let all run to ruin." It was the fight of his life, and if he lost, Christian civilization would slip into "rifling and robbery, murder and mischief, and plain insurrection."[6]

It never crossed More's mind that the simple power of scripture, when searched in the light of the Holy Spirit, produced a love for the Savior that directed a faithful life in the ways of righteousness. Tyndale trusted the plain power of God's words, for he worked in them every day. He spoke for the free flow of the Holy Spirit, which would teach the true meaning of God's word. As Nephi testified, "The words of Christ will tell you all things what ye should do" (2 Nephi 32:3). Tyndale would have smiled at that marvelous sentence, both in its sentiment and sound.

For Sir Thomas, however, the traditions of the church, the statements of the pope, and the writings of the church fathers were of higher authority than that of the scriptures. The church could not err! All who opposed her were heretics and worthy of temporal and eternal fires.

We get a sense of the issues involved by reflecting on the discussions that might be generated in a modern church setting concerning the authority of the living prophet, the Twelve Apostles, and other general authorities in comparison with the standard works. Five hundred years ago, such discussions split Europe. Because a living voice superseded scripture, More supported the pope. Scripture was open to numerous interpretations, and authority was needed to clarify its meaning. Only a living voice could do that, and it belonged to the bishop of Rome. Popes and cardinals live and die, Tyndale countered, but the scriptures remain forever. By what standard can we judge the statements of living authorities if not by that of the scriptures? In God's wisdom, he provided for the safeguarding of doctrine by a combination of both.

More's invective lashed out particularly at Tyndale's New Testament. "The faults be as ye see so many and so spread through the whole book, that likewise as it were as soon done to weave a new

Sir Thomas More.

web of cloth as to sew up every hole in a net, so were it almost as little labour and less to translate the whole book all new, as to make in his translation so many changes as need must ere it were made good."[7] Given that Tyndale's work is the foundation of the English Bible—the greatest literary masterpiece in world history—and that he is recognized as the world's most accomplished translator, not to mention a creator of modern English, More's self-inflicted blindness is cause for sorrow and reflection. A less prejudiced mind would have seen immediately the genius of what Tyndale had accomplished.

More, like Bishop Tunstall and others, pounced on certain words he felt threatened the very pillars of Catholic faith. More objected to Tyndale's "elders" instead of "priests" (elders suggested a lay leadership), "congregation" instead of "church" (a congregation is a body of believers, not an official organization), "repentance" instead of "do penance" (repentance is an inner turning of the heart instead of an outward act imposed by priests), "acknowledge sins" rather than "confession" (to acknowledge is a private admitting of sins to God, not to the priest's confessional), "love" instead of "charity" (charity assumed the giving of alms), and "image" instead of "idol" (challenging statues and paintings decorating churches). For these sins of translation, Tyndale had to be silenced, for they struck at the ritual and financial base of the church. In the thickets of apostasy, sin produced a handsome profit. Yet Tyndale was true to the Greek original.

But Tyndale could learn from his enemy. He had always asked that his translations be reviewed, inviting those who could improve them to do so. The final product was the critical factor, not whose name was laid to the work. So in his 1534 New Testament, Tyndale included some of More's efforts at scriptural translation because he felt they were better.

"This Is My Dear Son"

In 1531, Tyndale responded with *An Answer unto Sir Thomas More's Dialogue*. The battle was one of authority. Was scripture or the clergy to have the last word on doctrine? Drawing his arguments from Paul, John, Peter, and Jesus, Tyndale supported his claims. More aimed at cleverness, Tyndale struck at clarity. More wrote copiously, Tyndale wrote succinctly. More spread anger, Tyndale spread truth. As Daniell stated, "Tyndale makes clear that his aim is to . . . purge not to destroy. He does not want to burn anyone alive, not even Master More."[8] With all of his sophistication, More was aware that his church did need reforming, but he refused to admit it. Tyndale knew More was defending the indefensible and called him to account.

As always, Tyndale took the opportunity to teach essential truths of the New Testament. He did not allow his sweetness of faith to be destroyed in the fury of his opponent's onslaught. Though he called Sir Thomas's attack "More's blind maze,"[9] kindness flowed from his words:

"God causeth the law to be preached unto us, and writeth it in our hearts, and maketh us by good reasons feel that the law is good, and ought to be kept. . . . And on the other side I feel there is no power in me to keep the law; whereupon it would shortly follow that I should despair, if I were not shortly holp [helped]. But God . . . setteth his son Jesus before me, and all his passion and death, and saith to me: 'This is my dear Son, and he hath prayed for thee, and hath suffered all this for thee; and for his sake I will forgive thee all that thou hast done against this good law, and I will heal thy flesh, and teach thee to keep this law, if thou wilt learn. And I will bear with thee, and take all a worth that thou doest [all that you do will have value to me], till thou canst do better; and in the mean season, notwithstanding thy weakness, I will yet love thee no less than I do the angels in heaven, so thou wilt be diligent to learn. And I will assist thee, and keep thee, and defend thee, and be thy shield, and care for thee.' And the heart here beginneth to mollify and wax soft . . . and then, being overcome with this kindness, beginneth to love again and to submit herself unto the laws of God, to learn them and to walk in them."[10]

Are these the words of a dangerous heretic worthy of the fires of Smithfield? The tenderness between the Father and the Son and their love for us comes from deep within Tyndale's heart and is further shown in his translation of the Father's introduction of the Son. Tyndale rendered it, "Thou art my dear son in whom I delight," which is more intimate than the more formal King James version: "This is my beloved Son, in whom I am well pleased" (Matthew 3:17). The first version aims at the sweetness of the relationship, the second at the dignity surrounding it. Translation required difficult choices as well as help from the Holy Spirit.

Tyndale armed his readers with words to use when challenged concerning their faith. Its modern application for a Latter-day-Saint is apparent to every missionary in the field.

"When thou art asked why thou believest that thou shalt be saved through Christ, and of such like principles of our faith; answer, Thou wottest [knowest] and feelest that it is true. And when he asketh, How thou knowest that it is true; answer, Because it is written in thine heart. And if he ask who wrote it; answer, The Spirit of God. And if he ask how thou camest first by it; tell him . . . that inwardly thou wast taught by the Spirit of God . . . and . . . the Spirit of God . . . so testifieth unto thy soul."[11]

MORE COUNTERATTACKS

After writing his response, Tyndale had better things to do than conduct a word duel with a fellow scholastic. The Old Testament lay before him. People must know of David, Saul, Deborah, and Ruth. More had written, "For of the whole people, far more than four-tenths could never read English,"[12] yet Tyndale labored for those who could read. They could read the stories to each other until the nation as a whole became more literate. Though More attacked again, Tyndale left the arena for a greater fight. For Sir Thomas, this was the fight of his life. He must refute Tyndale, and he would work at it until his own martyrdom for the Catholic faith.

Responding to Tyndale's *Answer*, More struck again, writing the

voluminous *Confutation of Tyndale's Answer,* the longest religious diatribe in English. It was a cannon-blast of words. In this mammoth
of fury and religious justification, Tyndale was a "hell-hound in the
kennel of the devil . . . a drowsy drudge drinking deep in the devil's
dregs."[13] How More found time to write with his many duties as
chancellor inspires wonder. He spoke of losing "the rest of so many
nights' sleep" in his fight against heresy,[14] writing furiously by candlelight into the early hours of the morning. When he resigned, he
was still working on it.

More constructed his arguments with a lawyer's skill and a
zealot's fury, but he lacked the pure religion of Tyndale's contribution to the duel. Tyndale believed in a "feeling faith," as suggested
in his *Answer;* More defended a historical faith. *The Confutation* is
half a million words of shouting, so loud and long that it defeated
itself in its own swirl of rhetoric. It is a broadsword slashing with
invective at Tyndale's smaller rapier thrust. Tyndale rightly decided
to ignore it, but it serves as a reminder of the hurricane winds he
sailed against.

Few read More's massive polemic, but Sir Thomas did enrich the
English language in writing it. He introduced such words as *antici-
pate, meeting, monosyllable, obstruction, paradox, pretext, shuffle,* and
taunt, and such phrases as *not to see the wood for the trees, to make the
best of something, out of the frying pan into the fire,* and *a moon made
of green cheese.*[15]

"TREADING HERETICS UNDER OUR FEET LIKE ANTS"

In light of all Sir Thomas did to crush Tyndale, his translations,
and his friends, it is somewhat of a marvel to read what he said to
his son-in-law, Roper. It shows the greatness of mind he could have
nourished had it not been embittered by blind persecuting zeal. His
actions were beneath a man whose soul was in many ways as noble as
his foe's soul and whose courage was surely as deep. More's words

paint a prophetic vision that could have solved the religious intolerance that would plague Europe and America for centuries.

"Son Roper," he said, "I pray God that some of us, as high as we seem to sit upon the mountains treading heretics under our feet like ants, live not in the day that we gladly would wish to be at a league and composition with them to let them have their churches quietly to themselves, so that they would be content to let us have ours quietly to ourselves."[16]

In his *Utopia,* More believed there could be only one true religion. But in that work he affirmed that if men used reason, modesty, and good judgment, in the final analysis light would outshine darkness and all would recognize eternal truth. Sadly, in his fight with Tyndale, he did not follow his own model for an ideal society but reverted to the cruelty and darkness of past centuries.

As history's wheel turned the fortunes of men, More found himself in the down position. He courageously chose martyrdom at the hand of a king he had diligently served—the measure he had meted out to Tyndale's brethren. In prison, he experienced the fearful anticipation and haunting dreams of painful tortures that might come, for he wrote of "duress and hard handling" and "violent forcible ways."[17] Yet with lack of sympathy, he had approved of such pains upon others. He mocked the weakness of those recanting for fear of the fire but now discovered that "my flesh much more shrinking from pain and from death, than me thought it the part of a faithful Christian man."[18]

More claimed the right of free conscience, saying to his interrogators, "Me thinketh in good faith, that so were it good reason that every man should leave me to mine."[19] Nevertheless, this same privilege he had denied others. "My Lords, these terrors be arguments for children and not for me," he hurled back at his judges when threatened.[20] Yet he had used those same methods with inquisitorial skill.

"WE MAY YET MERRILY ALL MEET TOGETHER"

Did More see the irony of his position? He expressed delight upon hearing of the death of Zwingli, the Swiss reformer who, like

John Frith and William Tyndale, taught that the sacrament was a memorial only. On his epitaph, More chose to include that he was *molestus* (troublesome) to heretics.[21] In a letter to Erasmus, he explained this dark side of his nature. "I want to be as hateful to them as anyone can possibly be; for my increasing experience with these men frightens me with the thought of what the whole world will suffer at their hands."[22]

Perhaps fear was behind More's persecution—a fear that compromised his character. That he was proclaimed a Catholic saint astounds many. On the other hand, he wrote from his Tower prison:

"I will give counsel to every good friend of mine, but if he be put in such room, as to punish an evil man [who] lieth in his charge, by reason of his office, else leave the desire of punishing unto God and unto such other folk, as are so grown dead in charity, and so far cleave to God, that no secret, shrewd cruel affection, under the cloak of a just and a virtuous zeal, can creep in and undermine them. But let us that are no better than men of a mean [average] sort, ever pray for such merciful amendment in other folk, as our own conscience showeth us that we have need in ourself."[23]

Perhaps life in the last hour had taught More the introspection and mercy he needed to go to his death with the Christian soul he had lost in his war with Tyndale. We see him climbing the steps of his scaffold to a more humane death of beheading, thanks to the mercy of the king. How did he feel as he looked at Humphrey Monmouth, Tyndale's friend whom he had once locked in the Tower but who now, as a London sheriff, escorted him to his execution? We cannot help but wonder and hope that More's final words at the trial that condemned him will apply to a future meeting with William Tyndale at the bar of Christ, at which both men will stand:

"More have I not to say, my lords, but like as the blessed apostle Saint Paul, as we read in the Acts of the Apostles, was present and consented to the death of Saint Stephen, and kept their clothes that stoned him to death, and yet be they now both twain holy saints in heaven, and shall continue there friends forever, so I verily trust, and shall therefore right heartily pray, that though your lordships have now here in earth been judges to my condemnation, we may yet hereafter in heaven merrily all meet together, to our everlasting salvation."[24]

NOTES

1. Ackroyd, *Life of Thomas More*, 259; spelling standardized.
2. Roper, *Life of Sir Thomas More*, 198–99.
3. Bolt, *A Man for All Seasons*, v.
4. Mozley, *William Tyndale*, 164; emphasis added.
5. Daniell, *William Tyndale*, 261–62.
6. Moynahan, *God's Bestseller*, 172.
7. More, *Complete Works of St. Thomas More*, 6:292–93.
8. Daniell, *William Tyndale*, 271.
9. Duffield, *Work of William Tyndale*, 370.
10. Ibid., 369.
11. Greenslade, *Work of William Tindale*, 151–52.
12. Campbell, *Erasmus, Tyndale, and More*, 139.
13. Daniell, *William Tyndale*, 277.
14. Roper, *Life of Sir Thomas More*, 222.
15. Ackroyd, *Life of Thomas More*, 282.
16. Roper, *Life of Sir Thomas More*, 216.
17. Ackroyd, *Life of Thomas More*, 367; spelling standardized.
18. Ibid.; spelling standardized.
19. Ibid., 363; spelling standardized.
20. Roper, *Life of Sir Thomas More*, 234.
21. Ackroyd, *Life of Thomas More*, 275.
22. Moynahan, *God's Bestseller*, 274.
23. Campbell, *Erasmus, Tyndale, and More*, 265–66.
24. Roper, *Life of Sir Thomas More*, 250.

1531–1534
ENGLISH HOUSE, ANTWERP

PIRATED EDITIONS AND PROMISED REVISIONS

The scripture hath a body without, and within a soul, spirit, and life. It hath without a bark, a shell, and as it were an hard bone, for the fleshly minded to gnaw upon: and within it hath pith, ker-nel, marrow, and all sweetness for God's elect, which he hath chosen to give them his Spirit, and to write his law, and the faith of his Son, in their hearts.

—WILLIAM TYNDALE, "PROLOGUE TO THE PROPHET JONAS"

JONAH, JOHN, AND MATTHEW

Having been distracted by his duel with Sir Thomas More, Tyndale returned to his heart's obsession, translating the scriptures and teaching their truths to his fellowmen. In 1531, he translated the book of Jonah. The book's purpose, Tyndale wrote in a prologue, was to set before the reader a "sure earnest that God will even so deal with us, as he did with them, in all infirmi-ties, in all temptations, and in all like cases and chances."[1]

The book of Jonah was a favorite with the reformers because it emphasized God's mercy, both for Jonah and the sinful city of Nineveh. As a similitude for the sacrifice of Christ, it fit neatly into Tyndale's view of the totality of the witness for Christ found in both the New Testament and the Old Testament. Book burnings destroyed many of Tyndale's translations, and for centuries his Jonah translation was lost. But a single copy was found in 1861, which is now in the British Library. The King James Version of Jonah is based on Tyndale's work.

177

Tyndale also wrote *An Exposition upon the First Epistle of John* and then an *Exposition upon the V, VI, VII Chapters of Matthew* (the Sermon on the Mount). Tyndale's explanations offer insight into the essence of scripture. For example, notice his commentary on a verse from the Sermon on the Mount: "The preciousest gift that a man hath of God in this world is the true heart of his wife, to abide by him in wealth and woe, and to bear all fortunes with him. . . . Let every man have his wife, and think her the fairest and the best-conditioned, and every woman her husband so too. For God hath blessed thy wife, and made her without sin to thee, which ought to seem a beautiful fairness."[2] His comments on ostentatious displays of charity, prayers, or fasting contain the pithy wisdom of the common man: "If a peacock did look well on his feet, and mark the evil-favoured shrieking of his voice, he would not be so proud of the beauty of his tail."[3]

GEORGE JOYE'S PIRACY

Tyndale focused his major efforts on the Bible text. The word of God deserved his finest honing skills, and in 1534 he put forth revisions of the New Testament and Genesis. Tyndale did not divide his work into verses, which would appear a few decades after his death with publication of the Geneva Bible. In his 1526 edition, he begged the reader to forgive his faults, indicating that he would try to improve the translation. He was now diligently working on improvements. Like his other versions, the 1534 edition was a small six-by-four-inch book less than two inches thick. It was perfect for secreting in bales of cloth or bags of grain, and it was easy to hide at home.

In almost all areas of his life, Tyndale faced opposition. The market for Bibles in England was great, and some Dutch printers approached George Joye, another English exile, to produce a new version. Claiming that he had waited for Tyndale to revise his own copy and that Tyndale delayed, Joye put forward his own edition. Pirated printings had already appeared, but Joye changed words in Tyndale's translation that were critically important to him, rendering, for example, "life after life" instead of "resurrection," and failing to put his own name on the new translation.

This was too much for Tyndale, who was already under constant scrutiny for every word he translated. The legitimacy of his work was in danger. He disliked contention and favored letting the issue drop without comment, as he had "done divers other in time past."[4] But he published a note to his readers, explaining his disappointment at Joye's plagiarism and his unwarranted changes. This was well before copyright laws, and pirating another man's work was common if money could be made. Tyndale ascribed Joye's actions to "a little spice of covetousness and vainglory (two blind guides) . . . about which things I strive with no man."[5] Though Tyndale preferred not to divide the small community of English reformers, the dignity of the work required that Joye stand to account.

"I challenge George Joye," Tyndale wrote, "that he did not put his own name thereto and call it rather his own translation: and that he playeth bo peep, and in some of his books putteth in his name and title, and in some keepeth it out. It is lawful for who will to translate and show his mind, though a thousand had translated before him. But it is not lawful (thinketh me) nor yet expedient for the edifying of the unity of the faith of Christ, that whosoever will, shall by his own authority, take another man's translation and put out and in and change at pleasure, and call it a correction."[6]

Even the small group of exiled reformers faced threats to their unity. Joye tried dragging Tyndale into a prolonged quarrel, but he misjudged his man. As with More, once Tyndale had set the record straight, he went forward with his translating, letting his opponent fume and fuss without responding in kind. "Malice and envy are his two blind guides," Joye flung back. "Does Tyndale think his version cannot be improved? He must be the Almighty himself."[7] Despite his fuming, Joye could not bring Tyndale back into the fray.

Joye reveals an interesting detail about Tyndale's secretive life. He writes of a conversation the two men had while they walked in a field. Earlier, Tyndale had arranged to meet Stephen Vaughan outside the city walls. Apparently, even among other exiles, Tyndale was cautious, hesitating to reveal his actual place of abode if he had the slightest doubt about the loyalty of the person concerned.

THE 1534 REVISION

Tyndale's revised New Testament contained roughly five thousand changes. Many of them render the text not only closer to the original Greek but also more resonant in English. "Senior" became the familiar "elder." The word suggests someone who is wise and experienced and is an appropriate title for the Twelve Apostles. "Blessed are the maintainers of peace" is much improved by the simpler "peacemakers." His original "In the beginning was *that* word" flowed better as "In the beginning was *the* word," a change Tyndale received from Sir Thomas More. "There is no prophet without honor" sounds much stronger when translated, "A prophet is not without honour." Having created the word "birthright" in his Old Testament translation of 1530, Tyndale now used it in Hebrews instead of the long and clumsy "his right that belonged unto him in that he was the eldest brother."[8]

The tragedy of Tyndale's martyrdom is heightened by the realization that he would have continued to improve his translation in the coming years as well as given us a complete Old Testament. Like Joseph Smith, he barely saw forty years before he was taken.

A TASTE OF WHAT WE LOST

We do get some idea of what Tyndale would have done with the prophets had he lived, for he included in the back of his 1534 edition his translation of forty passages read during services at Salisbury Cathedral, many from the prophet Isaiah.[9] Comparing a few of them with the King James Version gives us an inkling of what we lost.

Isaiah 11:2, 4

KJV: The spirit of knowledge and of the fear of the Lord. But with righteousness shall he judge the poor.

Tyndale: The spirit of knowledge and of reverence. But he shall judge the causes of the poor with righteousness.

Do we fear the Lord or reverence him? Is it the poor who are to be judged or their causes?

Isaiah 58:3, 6–7

KJV: Behold, in the day of your fast ye find pleasure, and exact all your labours. . . . Is not this the fast that I have chosen? to loose the bands of wickedness, to undo the heavy burdens, and to let the oppressed go free, and that ye break every yoke? Is it not to deal thy bread to the hungry, and that thou bring the poor that are cast out to thy house?

Tyndale: Behold when ye fast, ye can find your own lusts, and can call cruelly on all your debtors. . . . Or is not this rather the fast that I have chosen? To loose wicked bonds and to unbind bundles of oppression? And to let the bruised go free? And that ye should break all manner of yokes? yea and to break the bread to the hungry, and to bring the poor that are harbourless unto thy house.

Notice Tyndale's craftsmanship of sound. We hear the alliteration of "can call cruelly . . . all" (both the "c" and "ll" sounds), of "bonds . . . unbind bundles . . . bruised . . . break the bread . . . bring" (the first three words end with "nd"; the last four begin with "br"), and of "harbourless . . . house" (the initial "h" and ending "s" sounds). As far as understanding the passage, there is no doubt in Tyndale that the heavy burden is debt that God expects the creditors to remit and that the "lusts" center on money. Breaking bread is more inclusive of the poor than the more distant "deal thy bread," and "harbourless" leaves no doubt that the poor are homeless instead of "cast out." In addition, a nice linkage occurs between "breaking" yokes and "breaking" bread that is lost in the KJV.

Isaiah 60:1–2

> **KJV:** Arise, shine; for thy light is come, and the glory of the Lord is risen upon thee. For behold, the darkness shall cover the earth, and gross darkness the people: but the Lord shall arise upon thee, and his glory shall be seen upon thee.
>
> **Tyndale:** Up, and receive light Jerusalem: for thy light is come, and the glory of the Lord is up over thee. For behold, darkness shall cover the earth, and a thick mist the nations. But the Lord shall rise as the sun over thee, and his glory shall be seen upon thee.

The image in this passage is much more obvious in Tyndale. We are to visualize a sunrise over an awakening city. "Up" shows an urgency missing in the statelier "arise." The nation is sleeping in the darkness, covered by a thick mist (the darkness and mist of apostasy). But the sun has risen, and the people must wake up, for God's light is already shining on them for the entire world to see. We can more readily visualize "a thick mist" (a heavy morning fog) than the rather obscure "gross darkness." In the KJV, we can miss the image of a sunrise completely. Tyndale makes sure we catch it.

Isaiah's most famous passage is found in chapter 53, which contains a wonderful description of the Savior's atonement. A few examples show how Tyndale aims at clarity. The prophets are difficult, and even more difficult without using the correct English words.

Isaiah 53

> **KJV:** He hath no form nor comeliness (v. 2).
> **Tyndale:** There was neither fashion or beauty on him.

KJV: Who shall declare his generation? (v. 8).
Tyndale: His generation who can number [them]?

KJV: He is cut off out of the land of the living (v. 8).
Tyndale: He is taken from the earth of living men.

KJV: Yet it pleased the Lord to bruise him; he hath put him to grief: when thou shalt make his soul an offering for sin, he shall see his seed, he shall prolong his days, and the pleasure of the Lord shall prosper in his hand (v. 10).

Tyndale: And yet the Lord determined to bruise him with infirmities. His soul giving herself for transgression, he shall see seed of long continuance, and the will of the Lord shall prosper in his hand.

KJV: By his knowledge shall my righteous servant justify many (v. 11).

Tyndale: With his knowledge, he being just, shall justify my servants and that a great number.

In almost every case, Tyndale is more readily understood, and the poetry of the sentence is easier on the ear. Tyndale makes Malachi's prophecy, so important to Latter-day-Saints, easier to grasp.

Malachi 3:2

KJV: But who may abide the day of his coming? and who shall stand when he appeareth?

Tyndale: Who shall endure in the day of his coming, or who shall stand to behold him?

A case could be made that the three committees that created the King James Version improved on Tyndale in a number of places ("pearl of great price" is preferable to "precious pearl," for instance). Tyndale would have acknowledged as much. Yet prolonged and consistent genius is rarely displayed in committees. It is an individual endowment, and without a doubt Tyndale had a unique gift with ancient languages and with the rich cadences and vocabulary of the English language.

WASTED BRIBE MONEY

Tyndale's 1534 New Testament had a print run of three thousand. Within a month, as testimony to the demand in England, another edition was printed. Meanwhile, the search for Tyndale continued. An English agent named Thomas Elyot was trying to apprehend Tyndale and whisk him secretly to England. Unable to arrest and extradite him through cooperation with officials from the Low Countries, Elyot decided to try kidnapping. He was armed with bribe money, but Tyndale's friends were true.

In 1532, Elyot wrote about his efforts: "The king willeth me, by his grace's letters, to remain at Brussels some space of time for the apprehension of Tyndale, which somewhat minisheth my hope of soon return; considering that, like as he is in wit movable, semblably [similarly] so is his person uncertain to come by; and as far as I can perceive, hearing of the king's diligence in the apprehension of him, he withdraweth him into such places where he thinketh to be farthest out of danger."

By the end of the year, Elyot had returned to England, broke from his many bribes. "I gave many rewards,"[10] he lamented, but to no avail. It was going to be very difficult, Elyot affirmed, to catch a man "venerated almost as an apostle."[11]

Tyndale settled into the English House in Antwerp under the patronage of Thomas Poyntz during the last months of his freedom. He received a generous stipend, and for the first time in years his needs were adequately met. Ironically, it was Sir Thomas More who earlier in his career represented the English merchants, obtaining certain areas in the city for them to trade. Now those efforts yielded protection for Tyndale.[12] The city authorities would be loath to violate the status of such a powerful group and jeopardize the economic well-being of the city.

ANTWERP'S LESS-FRIENDLY EYES

Antwerp also harbored less-friendly eyes. Early in 1533, a letter from a number of citizens to the chancellor of Brabant complained of Lutheranism in the town. It accused certain printers of producing offending materials and blamed city leaders for being complacent about heresy. The letter named names as well as locations used for hiding and preaching. An allusion in the letter surely refers to Tyndale:

"There is a printer at Antwerp, dwelling in the Camerstrate, within the old gate, next to the Vette Henne, on the same side, towards the churchyard of our lady. There shall you find books full of heresy in the English tongue, and also others; but you must go into the chamber within, and open the chests; there shall you find them. And the better to do so, take with you a Christian [Catholic] Englishman. And this printer will also show you a great heretic and doctor, who for his heresy has been driven out of England. . . . We beg you to act. . . . We write because our spiritual and lay heads have no care for these things."[13]

The writers urged a purging of Antwerp like that in Spain, where the cruelty of the Inquisition reached legendary status. The letter had its desired effect, though Tyndale remained cautiously at large. Authorities made arrests and delivered punishment, including executions. Despite ever-present danger, Tyndale carried on. Foxe provides this view of Tyndale's private life during his last months of freedom:

"He was a man very frugal and spare of body, a great student, an earnest labourer in the setting forth of the scriptures of God. He reserved or hallowed to himself two days in the week, which he named his pastime, Monday and Saturday. On Monday he visited all such poor men and women, as were fled out of England, by reason of persecution, into Antwerp; and these, once well understanding their good exercises and qualities, he did very liberally comfort and relieve; and in like manner provided for the sick and diseased persons. On the Saturday he walked round about the town, seeking every corner and hole, where he suspected any poor person to dwell; and where he found any to be well occupied, and yet over-burdened with children, or else were aged and weak, these also he plentifully relieved. And thus he spent his two days of pastime, as he called them. And truly his alms were very large, and so they might well be; for his exhibition that he had yearly of the English merchants at Antwerp, when living there, was considerable; and that, for the most part, he bestowed upon the poor. The rest of the days of the week he gave wholly to his book, wherein he most diligently travailed. When the Sunday came, then went he to some one merchant's chamber or other, whither came many other merchants, and unto them would he read some one parcel of scripture: the which proceeded so fruitfully, sweetly, and gently from him, much like to the writing of John the evangelist, that it was a heavenly comfort and joy to the audience to hear him read the scriptures; likewise, after dinner, he spent an hour in the same manner. He was a man without any spot or blemish of rancour or malice, full of mercy and compassion, so that no man living was able to reprove him of any sin or crime."[14]

A WIND CHANGE IN ENGLAND

During this time, Tyndale met and converted the chaplain of the English House, John Rogers. Rogers was loyal to the Catholic faith when he came from England in 1534, but he leaned toward the reformers. In Antwerp, his transformation became complete as he began to help Tyndale. Rogers would become a vital link in preserving the scriptural heritage Tyndale gave to the world.

Tyndale, though still in a city that breathed with danger, had time and means to refine his Hebrew. He began now to methodically move through the history books. Joshua, Judges, Ruth, and the books of Samuel flowed through his mind as he labored to give English life and voice to Samson, Naomi, David, Hannah, and Solomon.

Back in England, Henry VIII, relying on the efficiency of

Cromwell and Bishop Cranmer, broke with the papacy and became supreme head of the English church. Anne Boleyn, who once showed Tyndale's *Obedience of a Christian Man* to the king and who owned a beautiful vellum (calfskin or lambskin) edition of Tyndale's 1534 New Testament, was queen of England. In December, the convocation of Canterbury passed a resolution asking Henry to allow an English translation of the scriptures. Though nothing resulted from the petition (no one was willing to do the work), the resolution indicated a shift in thinking. The winds were changing, but they still blew ill will.

NOTES

1. Duffield, *Work of William Tyndale,* 87.
2. Ibid., 228, 229.
3. Ibid., 252.
4. Daniell, *Tyndale's New Testament,* 13.
5. Ibid.
6. Ibid., 13–14.
7. Mozley, *William Tyndale,* 280–81.
8. See ibid., 287–92, for other examples.
9. All of the Tyndale passages come from his 1534 New Testament, edited by David Daniell.
10. Mozley, *William Tyndale,* 240.
11. Bobrick, *Wide As the Waters,* 133.
12. Ackroyd, *Life of Thomas More,* 127–28.
13. Mozley, *William Tyndale,* 261–62.
14. Ibid., 264–65.

1535

ANTWERP AND VILVORDE CASTLE

"THE WILY SUBTLETIES OF THIS WORLD"

𝔐oreober 𝔍 take 𝔊od, which alone seeth the heart, to record to my conscience, beseeching him that my part be not in the blood of 𝔠hrist, if 𝔍 wrote, of all that 𝔍 habe written throughout all my book, aught of an ebil purpose, of enby or malice to any man, or to stir up any false doctrine or opinion in the church of 𝔠hrist, or to be author of any sect, or to draw disciples after me, or that 𝔍 would be esteemed, or had in price, above the least child that is born, sabe only of pity and compassion 𝔍 had, and yet habe, on the blindness of my brethren, and to bring them unto the knowl- edge of 𝔠hrist, and to make eberyone of them, if it were possible, as perfect as an angel of heaben.

—WILLIAM TYNDALE, "TO THE CHRISTIAN
READER" (1534 NEW TESTAMENT)

WARNING!

𝔈arly in 1535, Tyndale was living with Thomas Poyntz in the English House in Antwerp, contentedly working on the Old Testament. He was at the peak of his skills, and all portents pointed to the fulfillment of his dream. The fire in the bones had increased over the years, and the word of God flowed smoothly from his pen into powerful English. In May, warning of a new plot to capture him surfaced among the merchants. At the beginning of the month, George Collins, a merchant from London visiting Antwerp, wrote a letter to a fellow businessman regarding important

189

information he had recently received through the Christian Brethren's underground connections.

"Sir," he wrote, "it may please you to understand that the stadholder [viceroy] of Barrow spake with Mr. Flegge in the church, and he said: Mr. Flegge, there is commission come from the procuror-general of Brussels to take three Englishmen, whereof one is Dr. Barnes. Notwithstanding the stadholder said: We would be loth to do anything which were displeasure to the company [the merchant adventurers]. Wherefore he willeth Mr. Flegge to give Mr. Doctor warning."[1]

Brussels was firmly in the grasp of the Catholics. If Tyndale could be lured out of Antwerp, away from the privileges of the English House, or somehow be placed in the hands of the procurer-general of Brussels, his merchant friends would be powerless to save him. The secret meeting in the church with Robert Flegge, an English merchant, was probably not unique. Warnings invariably must have come before.

Robert Barnes was the Englishman who had carried a bundle of sticks at St. Paul's Cross in 1526 with the German merchants caught in Sir Thomas More's raid on the Steelyard. He was also the Englishman given safe conduct to England by Henry VIII—safe conduct that More wished to ignore so he could send Barnes to the stake. It is not surprising that he was a wanted man. But who were the other two the Brussels authorities were after?

"Mr. Flegge took so great kindness withal," Collins continued in his letter, "that he forgot to know who the other two persons shall be. By my next letter I shall write you what be the names of the other two persons. I pray you, show Mr. Doctor hereof."[2] So the other two, for the time being, remained unknown. It is not hard to guess who they were. George Joye and William Tyndale were producing the majority of heretical books, and Tyndale, in particular, was considered the head of the English reformers. Did they receive warning? Joye escaped to Calais, France, in late May or early June. Barnes was not in Antwerp at the time and was, therefore, the least of the three who needed warning. Tyndale, unwilling to leave

Antwerp and trusting that his friends in the city would have advance notice of an arresting party from Brussels, chose to remain. Besides, the semidiplomatic immunity enjoyed in the English House was a security he had rarely enjoyed. Antwerp's location was ideal for shipping his latest translation of the New Testament to England, and he knew the printers. He had lived a life of danger, so why should this latest threat pose any new significant problems? But the new threat was an ominous one. His unknown stalker was at that very moment enjoying Tyndale's unchallenged confidence.

Henry Phillips, the English Judas

The man behind Tyndale's capture was an Englishman named Henry Phillips.[3] Foxe devoted a large portion of Tyndale's life to Phillips's duplicity, receiving details of Tyndale's arrest from Thomas Poyntz,[4] who had been an eyewitness.

"William Tyndale, being in the town of Antwerp, had been lodged about one whole year in the house of Thomas Poyntz . . . about which time came thither one out of England, whose name was Henry Phillips . . . a comely fellow, like as he had been a gentleman, having a servant with him: but wherefore he came, or for what purpose he was sent thither, no man could tell."[5]

Phillips's purpose was malice and treachery. He hailed from a noble family, the third son of Richard Phillips, who was a member of Parliament. Educated at Oxford, he was apparently schooled for an ecclesiastical position and claimed high church patronage. He had troublesome habits, gambling being one of them. While transporting a large sum of money to London for his father, he lost it all to this vice. Afraid to go home, he sought money from a number of sources but without much luck. His letters home, written after his betrayal of Tyndale, reveal his desperate poverty, fawning entreaties, and bitter complaints. Evidence shows that he was easy to dislike.

When Phillips showed up in Louvain, a Catholic stronghold near Antwerp, he no longer had money problems. Because Louvain had a university, Phillips could claim scholarly interests to cover his motives. He found supporters in England with a lot of money willing to finance a betrayal. He intended to veil the watchful eyes looking after Tyndale in the English House, gain his trust, and then arrange for his delivery to the procurer-general of Brussels. We do not know how he discovered Tyndale's location, but by feigning interest in the English Bible among the merchants, he hoped to eventually come in contact with his prey. To accomplish his plan, Phillips had to appear respectable and interested in Tyndale's work.

THE MYSTERIOUS PATRON

Who backed Phillips's scheme? We can rule out the English government. Cromwell saw Phillips as an enemy to England. Without exception, official correspondence condemned Phillips as a traitor who spoke loathingly of Henry VIII. Phillips was a strong advocate of Catholicism and was hostile to Henry's threat to church unity.

Phillips claimed to have church patronage in England, and Foxe indicated that the entrapment "was not done with small charges and expenses, from whomsoever it came."[6] An assessment of the leading bishops active in the persecution who had access to large sums of money points the finger at Bishop Stokesley of London. He had collaborated with More in several arrests and executions and had fiercely condemned Tyndale's writings, and he remained proud of his cruel treatment of heretics, even on his deathbed. His servant John Tisen, one of Tyndale's former pupils, just happened to be in Antwerp in 1533 on unknown business.

Phillips was in desperate financial stress in London, Stokesley's territory. He was known as an enemy to the new ideas coming from the Continent, and he had a reputation conducive to unsavory dealings. He was educated and could pass himself off, without suspicion, as interested in the scholarship of Tyndale's work. All Phillips needed to do was convince authorities in Brussels that he could deliver on his promise to catch the three leading reformers of the day, which he apparently accomplished, as Collins's letter indicates and subsequent events prove.

Suspicion also falls on Sir Thomas More, although he was in prison at the time of Tyndale's capture. Early in his imprisonment, he was indifferently watched, allowed visitors, and could have made necessary arrangements. His hatred for the reformers, particularly Tyndale, was venomous. His efforts led to the death of Tyndale's friend John Frith, and More continued to write against Tyndale even after his fall from Henry's favor. More had the finances to back Phillips, the contacts in Brussels, and the international influence needed to bring Phillips into contact with the authorities of the Low Countries. Later, while in Rome, Phillips claimed a special friendship with More.

It was Sir Thomas who earlier had probed deeply into Tyndale's personal habits. Who were his friends and supporters? Where was he living? How tall was he? How did he dress? What were his daily habits? More asked these questions of every captured heretic. He could have pieced together enough evidence to guess Tyndale's location with some accuracy.

Stokesley gave in to Cromwell's pressure and accepted Henry as head of the church in England. More did not. Stokesley hated heretics, but he never claimed a part in Tyndale's burning. More was beheaded before Tyndale came to trial. Perhaps More and Stokesley worked in concert. Without doubt, Sir Thomas was the more intelligent. He had used spies and informers before with great effectiveness, and he nursed the greater hatred. To capture Tyndale would have been the crowning achievement of his heresy hunting. Regardless of who provided the funding, the plan worked smoothly.

Cautious Inquiries

"Master Tyndale divers times was desired forth to dinner and supper amongst merchants; by means whereof this Henry Phillips became acquainted with him, so that within a short space Master Tyndale had a great confidence in him, and brought him to his lodging, to the house of Thomas Poyntz; and had him also once or twice with him to dinner and supper, and further entered such friendship with him, that through his procurement he lay in the same house of the said Poyntz; to whom he showed moreover his books, and other secrets of his study, so little did Tyndale then mistrust this traitor."[7]

But Thomas Poyntz was a practical businessman dedicated to the protection of his guest and accustomed to assessing men's characters. There was something about Phillips that aroused his anxiety.

"Poyntz, having no great confidence in the fellow, asked Master Tyndale how he came acquainted with this Phillips. Master Tyndale answered, that he was an honest man, handsomely learned, and very conformable [to reform beliefs]. Then Poyntz, perceiving that he bare such favour to him, said no more, thinking that he was brought acquainted with him by some friend of his."[8]

Phillips initially tried to sound out Poyntz's dedication to Tyndale. Perhaps with enough bribe money, Poyntz could be convinced to help with the scheme. It would certainly be easier to lure Tyndale into a trap if the merchant he trusted so completely could be engaged as Phillips's ally. And if Phillips could not persuade Poyntz, perhaps he could gain enough information from him to approach other English merchants. Tyndale dined with and taught these men. The possibility needed exploring.

"The said Phillips, being in the town three or four days, upon a time desired Poyntz to walk with him forth of the town . . . and in walking together without the town, had communication of divers things . . . by which talk Poyntz as yet suspected nothing, but after, by the sequel of the matter, he perceived more what he intended. . . . But after, when the time was past, Poyntz perceived this to be his mind, to feel if he could perceive by him, whether he might break with him in the matter, for lucre of money, to help him to his purpose, for he perceived before that he was monied, and would that Poyntz should think no less."[9]

His suggested hints not finding a ready ear, the cautious Phillips felt that bribes would not move the English merchants. On the contrary, if they suspected him they would surely warn Tyndale. Regrettably, Poyntz did not put the pieces together earlier or realize that anyone with connections to the Catholic university at Louvain could not be the reformer's ally.

Phillips soon learned that he could expect no help from the Antwerp authorities; nor should he risk asking for it. Any movement in that direction would result in a whispered warning in the back of a church or a discreet letter passed during a business transaction. "So it was to be suspected, that Phillips was in doubt to move this matter for his purpose, to any of the rulers or officers of the town of Antwerp, for doubt it should come to the knowledge of some Englishmen, and by the means thereof Master Tyndale should have had warning."[10]

THE TRAP

In Brussels, however, Phillips could find the allies he needed. "So Phillips went from Antwerp to the court of Brussels, which is from thence twenty-four English miles. . . . To make short, the said Phillips did so much there, that he procured to bring from thence with him to Antwerp, the procuror-general, who is the emperor's attorney, with certain other officers, as after followeth."[11]

Having procured his arresting party, Phillips now needed the right moment. Fearing the loyal and suspicious Poyntz, Phillips sent his servant to inquire if Tyndale was at the house. Poyntz was sitting by the door as the servant approached. For Phillips to catch his man, there must be no friend nearby to warn or protect him. Unfortunately for Tyndale, Poyntz soon needed to leave to attend to affairs in Barrois, a town eighteen miles away. He would be gone a number of weeks. Phillips's opportunity had arrived.

"In the time of his [Poyntz's] absence Henry Phillips came again . . . to the house of Poyntz, and coming in, spake with his wife, asking her for Master Tyndale. . . . Then went he forth again (as it is thought) to . . . set the officers whom he brought with him from Brussels, in the street, and about the door. Then about noon he came again, and went to Master Tyndale, and desired him to lend him forty shillings; 'for,' said he, 'I lost my purse this morning, coming over at the passage.' . . . So Master Tyndale took him forty shillings, which was easy to be had of him, if he had it; for in the wily subtleties of this world he was simple and inexpert."[12]

Calmly and in the sincerest of voices, Phillips asked for money from the man whom he was about to betray. He had lost his purse but still desired to treat Tyndale to dinner. Could his generous friend not lend him enough for the day? Blood money from England, apparently, was not enough. Phillips would have the purse of Tyndale himself! Foxe's account continues to its inevitable conclusion:

"Then said Phillips, 'Master Tyndale! You shall be my guest here this day.' 'No,' said Master Tyndale, 'I go forth this day to dinner, and you shall go with me, and be my guest, where you shall be welcome.' So when it was dinner-time, Master Tyndale went forth with Phillips, and at the going forth of Poyntz's house, was a long narrow entry, so that two could not go in a front. Master Tyndale would have put Phillips before him, but Phillips would in no wise, but put Master Tyndale before, for that he pretended to show great humanity. So Master Tyndale, being a man of no great stature, went before, and Phillips, a tall comely person, followed behind him; who had set officers on either side of the door upon two seats, who, being there, might see who came in the entry; and coming through the same entry, Phillips pointed with his finger over Master Tyndale's head down to him, that the officers who sat at the door might see that it was he whom they should take."[13]

There was no Poyntz sitting at the door to save him, but Tyndale noticed the officers at the last minute. Suspecting a trap, he tried to back down the narrow entrance and return to the house. Phillips had foreseen that possibility and insisted that Tyndale go first. "Nay, said Phillips, by your leave you shall go forth; and by force bare him forward upon the officers."[14]

And so William Tyndale was taken on May 21, 1535.

PRECIOUS RESCUED MANUSCRIPTS

For a decade, Tyndale had eluded his enemies. Now, betrayed by a perceived friend, he gave up without a struggle. Seeing his resignation, his captors were touched by his innocence. Speaking later to Poyntz, the officers indicated "that they pitied to see his simplicity when they took him." Regardless of their emotions, they "brought him to the emperor's attorney, or procuror-general. . . . Then came the procuror-general to the house of Poyntz, and sent away all that was there of Master Tyndale's, as well his books as other things; and from thence Tyndale was had to the castle of Filford [Vilvorde], eighteen English miles from Antwerp, and there he remained until he was put to death."[15]

Fortunately, a period of time intervened between Tyndale's arrest and the confiscation of his books. He was working on the Old Testament, and his friend John Rogers later used his manuscript in publishing Matthew's Bible. Several treatises were also published after Tyndale's death, one on the sacrament that paralleled Frith's views. Were these precious manuscripts already hidden, or did Poyntz's wife quickly hide them before the searchers returned to gather evidence? Tyndale had shown Phillips "his books, and other secrets of his study," so he knew where to send the searchers and what to look for. There is some satisfaction in visualizing Phillips's disappointment in not finding Tyndale's manuscripts. We do not know who saved Joshua through Chronicles, but John Rogers made ready use of them. Soon they were circulating freely in England. The man was snared, but his work continued.

NOTES

1. Mozley, *William Tyndale*, 307.
2. Ibid., 307–8.
3. Spelled Philips in some sources but standardized here as Phillips.
4. Spelled Pointz in some sources but standardized here as Poyntz.
5. Foxe, *Acts and Monuments*, 5:121–22.
6. Ibid., 5:123.
7. Ibid., 5:122.
8. Ibid.
9. Ibid.

10. Ibid.
11. Ibid., 5:122–23.
12. Ibid., 5:123.
13. Ibid.
14. Foxe's preface to Daye's folio, as quoted in Mozley, 297 n.
15. Foxe, *Acts and Monuments,* 5:123.

"A YEAR AND ONE HUNDRED THIRTY-FIVE DAYS"

The poor and wretched sinner feeleth so great mercy, love and kindness in God, that he is sure in himself how that it is not possible that God should forsake him, or withdraw his mercy and love from him; and boldly crieth out . . . What shall make me believe that God loveth me not? Shall tribulation? Anguish? Persecution? Shall hunger? Nakedness? Shall sword? Nay. . . . In all such tribulations a Christian man perceiveth that God is his Father, and loveth him even as he loved Christ when he shed his blood on the cross.

—WILLIAM TYNDALE, *A PATHWAY INTO THE HOLY SCRIPTURE*

THE DARK PRISON OF VILVORDE CASTLE

The account records of the Castle of Vilvorde are preserved in the archives of Brussels. Under the title "Account of the confiscated goods of the Lutherans and heretical sects," we read the following entry concerning funds paid to Adolf van Wesele, lieutenant of the castle: "In keeping of a certain prisoner, named Willem Tintalus, Lutheran . . . for a year and one hundred thirty-five days, at forty stivers the day." Tyndale paid for his own imprisonment, and his goods were used to that purpose.

Though Tyndale was not a Lutheran, his defense of salvation through faith in Christ, not the rituals of Catholicism, bound him to that initial reformer. He was a heretic, and as a heretic he would be confined and tried. He was now in the hands of the Holy Roman Emperor, Charles V, and Charles was a devout Catholic. Under his rule and that of his son Phillip, the Spanish Inquisition would continue its cruel march into historical infamy. Clearly things looked dark.

Vilvorde Castle was built in 1374 of great strength. Its seven towers looked down upon an encircling moat. Entrance was through one of three drawbridges. The castle was damp with a perpetual musty smell; in the winters it was cold and dark. It no longer stands, but in Tyndale's day it served as the main prison for the Low Countries.

Tyndale was closely confined, his only visitors those hostile to him. He was a noted prisoner, and it would not do to have him escape. Vilvorde was the logical choice both in proximity to Brussels and Louvain and in security. Tyndale passed his days in the castle's cheerless rooms, anticipating no leniency from his captors.

"It Is No Great Matter Whether They Be Guilty or Innocent"

Tyndale had friends among the English merchants and a powerful supporter in England in the person of Thomas Cromwell. He could not be lightly examined or executed. There was still hope, and Thomas Poyntz went to work to turn that hope into reality. Soon, "by the help of English merchants, were letters sent, in favour of Tyndale, to the court of Brussels. Also, not long after, letters were directed out of England to the council at Brussels, and sent to the merchant-adventurers, to Antwerp, commanding them to see that with speed they should be delivered."[1]

Poyntz was the lead man in all of these endeavors and was fighting an uphill battle. Charles V was not on good terms with England's Henry. His aunt was Catherine of Aragon, the wife Henry had just divorced to marry Anne Boleyn. Charles was also chafing from the rise of Lutheranism in Germany and his waning control over the German states. There was little hope of clemency from this quarter.

Tyndale's accuser, the procurer-general, was named Pierre

Dufief, a ruthless, cruel tormentor of Lutherans. If his religious fervor failed to motivate him to condemn Tyndale, his greed might, for the

procurer-general received a portion of a man's goods if he was found guilty. He was also paid a fee for his labor. In Tyndale's case, he received 128 pounds, a considerable sum for the time. For Dufief, the line between accuser and judge was thin, and he occupied both roles cunningly.

The commissioners assigned to judge Tyndale also detested charitable sentences, especially when the accused was a famous heretic. They found support in the Decree of Augsburg, which made the preaching of justification by faith a capital crime. To rid Europe of the acknowledged leader of the English Reformation would be a coup for the heresy haters. One of them, a theologian from the university at Louvain named James Masson, strongly opposed anything that challenged Catholicism, including the gentle criticisms of Erasmus.

A second commissioner, a professor at Louvain named Ruard Tapper, had experience in dealing with dissent. Nine months after Tyndale's death, the pope appointed Tapper inquisitor general for all of the Low Countries. Known for his cruelty and fanaticism, he was guided by a general rule that often typified the approach to justice: "It is no great matter whether they that die on account of religion be guilty or innocent, provided we terrify the people by such examples; which generally succeeds best, when persons eminent for learning, riches, nobility or high station are thus sacrificed."[2] Other less notorious men were also assigned to Tyndale's case, bringing the number to more than a dozen.

CROMWELL'S SPY

Letters to Brussels from English merchants would not have been treated lightly. The merchants made up a powerful economic force and could not be ignored. In their eyes, their diplomatic privileges had been compromised with Tyndale's arrest. Tyndale was honored among many of the English House for his religious beliefs; in addition, his translations and other writings were good for business, even if they needed to be clandestinely slipped into the English market.

Poyntz, in particular, was determined to do everything he could to save his friend. He personally carried letters throughout Belgium and to and from England. Merchant letters, combined with pressure from the English court, just might be enough to turn the tide in Tyndale's favor. Henry, however, did not want to be seen as supporting the reformers—support from his court came mainly from Anne Boleyn. Henry had broken with Rome and was merrily divesting the Catholic Church of much of its land in England, but he did not favor Lutheran ideas and had to walk a thin line. He executed Sir Thomas More and Bishop John Fisher, both staunch papists, but he also sent fourteen Anabaptist heretics to the stake within a few days of Tyndale's arrest. Unfortunately for Tyndale, they were Dutch. The powers in Brussels would not be inclined to release a notorious English heretic as a favor.

Cromwell had to be cautious, but he began to weave a judicious route through the uncertain world of 16th-century politics. He instructed his godson Thomas Theobald, whom he had used in diplomatic missions overseas, to gather information. In July 1535, Theobald was in Antwerp writing to Archbishop Thomas Cranmer and secretary Cromwell about Tyndale and Phillips. He had been to Louvain, met with Phillips, and gathered what insight he could. He wrote to Cranmer:

"All succour that I can perceive them to have, is only by him which hath taken Tyndale, called [Henry] Phillips, with whom I had a long and familiar communication; for I made him believe that I was minded to tarry and study at Louvain. I could not perceive the contrary by his communication, but that Tyndale shall die, which he doth follow [urge] and procureth with all diligent endeavor, rejoicing much therein. . . . This said Phillips is greatly afraid (insomuch as I can perceive) that the English merchants that be in Antwerp will lay watch to do him some displeasure privily.

Wherefore of truth he hath sold his books in Louvain . . . intending to go hence to Paris; and doth tarry here upon nothing but of the return of his servant, which he hath long since sent to England with letters; and by cause of his long tarrying he is marvelously afraid lest he be taken, and come into Mr. Secretary's [Cromwell] handling with his letters."[3]

Phillips undoubtedly sent his servant back to England to report on his success and receive money in payment. He feared both the vengeance of the merchants and the pursuit of Cromwell, for Phillips had spoken strongly against the king, and his letters, if found, would have been damaging evidence. Despite his fears, he remained to see Tyndale's prosecution through to the end. Had he fled, Phillips would have been unable to remove Tyndale's last hope.

Tyndale's Untiring Friend

Poyntz knew of Theobald's visit, but when nothing happened, he took matters into his own hands. Poyntz's brother John had a position at court and could, perhaps, use his influence to move matters in Tyndale's favor. Thomas wrote a poignant letter on August 25, urging his brother to persuade Cromwell to pressure Brussels to release Tyndale.

"Brother, I write to you on a matter greatly concerning the king. My love of my country and my duty to my prince compels me to speak, lest the king be misled and brought into injury by men, yes traitors, who, under colour of forwarding his honour, seek to bring their own purposes to pass. . . . For whereas it was said here the king had granted his gracious letters in the favour of one William Tyndale, for to have been sent hither; the which is in prison and like to suffer death, except it be through his gracious help; it is thought those letters be stopped. This man lodged with me three quarters of a year, and was taken out of my house by a sergeant-at-arms, otherwise called a door-warder, and the procuror-general of Brabant; the which was done by procurement out of England, and, as I suppose, unknown to the king's grace till it was done. For I know well, if it

203

had pleased his grace to have sent him a commandment to come into England, he would not have disobeyed it, to have put his life in jeopardy. . . .

"And by the means that this poor man, William Tyndale, hath lain in my house three quarters of a year, I know that the king has never a truer hearted subject to his grace this day living. . . . The death of this man will be a great hindrance to the gospel, and to the enemies of it one of the highest pleasures. . . . And I think he shall shortly be at a point to be condemned; for there are two Englishmen at Louvain that do and have applied it sore, taking great pains to translate out of English into Latin in those things that may make against him, so that the clergy here may understand it, and to condemn him, as they have done all others, for keeping opinions contrary to their business, the which they call the order of holy church.

"Brother, the knowledge that I have of this man causes me to write as my conscience bids me; for the king's grace should have of him at this day as high a treasure as of any one man living, that has been of no greater reputation. Therefore I desire you that this matter may be solicited to his grace for this man, with as good effect as shall lie in you, or by your means to be done, for in my conscience there be not many perfecter men this day living, as knows God. Brother, I think that if Walter Marsh, now being governor of the English house, had done his duty effectually here at this time, there would have been a remedy found for this man."[4]

Of all those who loved Tyndale and valued his work, none fought so earnestly and without concern for his own safety or affairs as did Thomas Poyntz. We sense his frustration with the head of the English House, whom Poyntz accused of dragging his feet for fear of appearances. Master Marsh had good reason not to pursue the release of Tyndale too actively, as the consequences for Poyntz later proved.

"To Know the King's Pleasure for Tyndale"

John Poyntz did as his brother asked and forwarded the letter to

Cromwell, but Cromwell had already acted. In one of Cromwell's "remembrances" preserved in the Records Office in England is an entry regarding one of his visits with the king. It reads, "To know the king's pleasure for Tyndale, and whether I shall write or not."[5] The visit took place in August; John Poyntz did not forward his brother's letter until September 21. Cromwell had already received permission from Henry and wrote two letters to highly placed members of the privy council in the Netherlands, asking clemency for Tyndale as a favor to the king of England—one to the council president, Archbishop Carondolet of Palermo, and a second to the Marquis of Bergen-op-Zoom, an official in the Netherlands.

Cromwell sent the letters to Stephen Vaughan, who was in London at the time. Vaughan had been impressed with Tyndale when the two met in Antwerp and could be counted on to help. Vaughan forwarded the letters to George Collins, who passed them on to his fellow merchant Robert Flegge. Earlier, Collins and Flegge had actively issued warnings about Henry Phillips's presence in the area. The Marquis of Bergen-op-Zoom was in Germany escorting the daughter of the king of Denmark to her marriage, so the ever-loyal Poyntz hurried after him. Overtaking him, he delivered Cromwell's letter, along with other letters written by the merchants, including one from Flegge, pleading for Tyndale.

The marquis reminded Poyntz that his own countrymen had recently been burned in England (fourteen Anabaptists), but Poyntz remained determined. If someone had spoken in their favor, he claimed, certainly England would not have denied a request for their release. The marquis then told Poyntz that he was a busy man, the princess was ready to leave, and he had no time to deal with the matter. Poyntz countered that he was prepared to accompany the marquis to his next stop, where the marquis could write the necessary letters. Poyntz was so solicitous that the marquis finally agreed. He composed three letters—one to the council itself, one to Cromwell, and one to the merchant adventurers in Antwerp.

Things looked brighter, and Poyntz rushed back with the precious documents. He hand delivered the letters to the emperor's council in Brussels and was told to wait for a reply. With the response in hand, he returned to Antwerp and was instructed by the merchants there to personally escort the reply and other letters back to England.

"And he, very desirous to have Master Tyndale out of prison, let not to take pains, with loss of time in his own business and occupying, and diligently followed with the said letters, which he there delivered to the council [in England], and was commanded by them to tarry until he had other letters, with which he was not dispatched thence in a month after. At length, the letters being delivered him, he returned again, and delivered them to the emperor's council at Brussels, and there tarried for answer of the same."[6] Poyntz knew the prosecution against Tyndale was proceeding. For a businessman used to prompt transactions, the grinding gears of diplomacy must have been agonizing.

TYNDALE TO BE RELEASED

The days continued to drag on endlessly. Tyndale had been in prison for five months while the two countries sparred over his future. Both Flegge and Foxe provide details of what then took place. Flegge wrote to Cromwell at the end of September, informing him of his efforts and adding that the marquis "is very sorry to be absent from court, and so unable to render the king's highness and you such service as he would wish; but he has written to the bishop of Palermo, begging him strongly to do everything to further your wishes; for he can do most in the matter. This letter from the marquis to the archbishop, together with your own letter to the same, the messenger has presented, and begged for a favourable and speedy answer. The archbishop spoke with the queen and council, and has written you the answer which I send by the same bearer. I pray God it may be to the king's pleasure and yours."[7]

Poyntz paced the halls of the council chambers for "three or four days." He had some reason to hope for the best; after all, Tyndale's writings were all directed toward the English. Strictly speaking, he had not troubled anyone in the Low Countries. He had not written in any language other than English, and the English government was pushing for his release, not his condemnation. Finally, "it was told him by one that belonged to the Chancery, that Master Tyndale should have been delivered to him according to the tenor of the letters."[8] He had won! Tyndale would soon be back at English House, and this time the security guarding him would not be breached.

Regrettably, Poyntz had not counted on the vindictiveness and influence of Henry Phillips, who, though deeply frightened by the merchants of Antwerp, had stayed on in the safer city of Brussels. Seeing Tyndale on the verge of release, Phillips, "doubting lest he should be put from his purpose, . . . knew no other remedy but to accuse Poyntz, saying, that he was a dweller in the town of Antwerp, and there had been a succourer of Tyndale, and was one of the same opinion; and that all this was only his own labour and suit, to have Master Tyndale at liberty, and no man's else. Thus upon his information and accusation, Poyntz was attached [arrested] by the procuror-general, the emperor's attorney, and delivered to the keeping of two sergeants at arms."[9]

POYNTZ ARRESTED

It was now November, and Tyndale's champion was under house arrest in Brussels. How Phillips must have gloated in his victory after taking great lengths to draw up twenty-four articles against Poyntz, who was soon fighting for his own life. For several months, the prosecutor grilled Poyntz, with Phillips always lurking in the background, just as he had done outside the door when Tyndale's examiners probed for damaging evidence they might use against him. Poyntz drew upon every strategy he could to delay but was finally cornered and entangled in the legal net of Dutch law. Unable to obtain release on bail through the Antwerp merchants, Poyntz could see death staring him in the face.

Before being taken to a strong prison like the one that held

Tyndale, Poyntz escaped. Hiding in the darkness of Brussels until morning light, he slipped through the opening city gates. Familiar with the countryside, he eluded his pursuers and finally made his way to England. His defense of Tyndale had left him financially ruined, and his Dutch wife refused to join him in England with her children. He had gambled all in behalf of the father of the English Bible and barely escaped with his life. Meanwhile, the loneliness of the dark rooms of Vilvorde Castle closed in around William Tyndale as he waited for his judges to pronounce his inevitable fate.

NOTES

1. Foxe, *Acts and Monuments,* 5:123–24.
2. Mozley, *William Tyndale,* 326.
3. Ibid., 304–5; spelling standardized.
4. Ibid., 309–11.
5. Ibid., 312.
6. Foxe, *Acts and Monuments,* 5:124.
7. Mozley, *William Tyndale,* 313.
8. Foxe, *Acts and Monuments,* 5:124.
9. Ibid.

"OPEN THE KING OF ENGLAND'S EYES!"

Here seest thou the uttermost, what a Christian man must look for. It is not enough to suffer for righteousness; but that no bitterness or poison be left out of thy cup, thou shalt be reviled and railed upon. . . . Well, though iniquity so highly prevail, and the truth, for which thou diest, be so low kept under, and be not once known before the world, insomuch that it seemeth rather to be hindered by thy death than furthered, (which is of all griefs the greatest) yet let not thine heart fail thee, neither despair, as though God had forsaken thee, or loved thee not: but comfort thyself with old ensamples, how God hath suffered all his old friends to be so entreated, and also his only and dear son Jesus; whose ensample, above all other, set before thine eyes, because thou art sure he was beloved above all other, that thou doubt not but thou art beloved also, and so much the more beloved, the more thou art like to the image of his ensample in suffering.

—WILLIAM TYNDALE, *EXPOSITION UPON THE V, VI, AND VII CHAPTERS OF MATTHEW*

"GREAT DISPUTATION TO AND FRO"

We know little about the year and one hundred and thirty-five days Tyndale spent in Vilvorde while Poyntz desperately attempted to save him. Masson and Tapper, the theologians from Louvain, engaged in many debates with him both in writing and in person. Dufief, the emperor's attorney, questioned him repeatedly over the months of his confinement. To be useful as evidence, Tyndale's writings had to be translated into Latin.

All of this took time, and so the days passed from summer into fall and then winter.

We do not know whether Tyndale learned of the efforts to save him. Under house arrest, Poyntz likely had little opportunity to communicate with Tyndale. The ever-hovering Phillips would have cast a constant dark shadow over deliberations regarding both men, and he is almost certainly one of the two Englishmen mentioned by Poyntz in a letter to his brother John who were engaged in translating Tyndale's works into Latin.

Though offered an advocate, Tyndale preferred to answer for himself and did so with such gentleness and charm that his examiners could not help but be moved by his patience and intelligence. He grounded his answers in the scripture. Masson and Tapper, both intelligent, readily recognized the mark of a sound mind. Foxe writes, "There was much writing and great disputation to and fro, between him and them of the university of Louvain . . . in such sort, that they all had enough to do, and more than they could well wield, to answer the authorities and testimonies of the Scripture, whereupon he most pithily grounded his doctrine."[1]

In his defense, Tyndale expounded the scriptures with "divers lawyers and doctors in divinity, as well as friars and others, with whom he had many conflicts."[2] He requested the presence of some divines who could speak his beloved English. The constant arguments in Latin tired him until the sound of his native tongue, even coming from an opponent, provided relief.

WINNING THE HEARTS OF HIS ENEMIES

Close association with Tyndale usually softened feelings against him. Even the cruel Dufief was softened by his conferences with him. Foxe writes, "The procurator-general, the emperor's attorney, being there, left his testimony of him, that he was, 'Homo doctus, pius et bonus,' that is [to say] 'a learned, a good, and a godly man.'"[3]

In this way, Tyndale resembled Joseph Smith, who often subdued the hearts of his enemies from Missouri to Carthage. And like

Paul in Philippi, Tyndale converted his jailors. "Such was the power of his doctrine, and the sincerity of his life, that during the time of his imprisonment (which endured a year and a half), it is said, he converted his keeper, the keeper's daughter, and others of his household. Also the rest that were with Tyndale conversant in the castle, reported of him that if he were not a good Christian man, they could not tell whom to trust."[4]

Delays continued during the exchange of letters in the summer and fall of 1535, and winter soon settled in on Tyndale. We have one precious letter he wrote from Vilvorde, which reveals the conditions he endured while the weary months wore on. He wrote it in the fall or early winter of 1535, obviously to someone in authority to ease his condition. Mozley renders the following translation from the original Latin:

"I believe, right worshipful, that you are not unaware of what may have been determined concerning me. Wherefore I beg your lordship, and that by the Lord Jesus, that if I am to remain here through the winter, you will request the commissary to have the kindness to send me, from the goods of mine which he has, a warmer cap; for I suffer greatly from cold in the head, and am afflicted by a perpetual catarrh [an inflammation of the nose and throat], which is much increased in this cell; a warmer coat also, for this which I have is very thin; a piece of cloth too to patch my leggings. My overcoat is worn out; my shirts are also worn out. He has a woollen shirt, if he will be good enough to send it. I have also with him leggings of thicker cloth to put on above; he has also warmer night caps. And I ask to be allowed to have a lamp in the evening; it is indeed wearisome sitting alone in the dark. But most of all I beg and beseech your clemency to be urgent with the commissary, that he will kindly permit me to have the Hebrew bible, Hebrew grammar, and Hebrew dictionary, that I may pass the time in that study. In return may you obtain what you most desire, so only that it be for the salvation of your soul. But if any other decision has been taken concerning me, to be carried out before winter, I will be patient, abiding the will of God, to the glory of the grace of my Lord Jesus Christ; whose Spirit (I pray) may ever direct your heart. Amen. W. Tindalus."[5]

The letter is a treasure for its portrayal of humanity in trial. Its dignity, courage, and grace, with no hint of fawning or criticism, no spirit of bitterness or accusation—only resignation to the will of God—has few equals. Tyndale's most earnest request was not for the warmer comforts that would prepare him for winter but for his Hebrew Bible, grammar, and dictionary so that he might continue his work and retain his skill with the language during his months of confinement. In like manner, Paul, while imprisoned in Rome, requested that Timothy bring him "the cloke that I left at Troas with Carpus, when thou comest, bring with thee, and the books, but especially the parchments" (2 Timothy 4:13).

We will never know if his requests were granted, but it is doubtful he received the Hebrew books that would allow him to continue the work for which he was a prisoner. He had an active mind, and the tedious days must have been as great a trial as the fear of his coming death.

STEPHEN VAUGHAN'S LAST APPEAL

One man remained who still felt that an attempt to free Tyndale might meet with success. Stephen Vaughan, who had earlier tried to convince Tyndale to return to England, wrote to Cromwell in April 1536, remarking, "If now you send me but your letter to the privy council, I could deliver Tyndale from the fire, so it come by time, for else it will be too late."[6]

Perhaps Cromwell, an efficient and practical man who knew the ins and outs of international politics, realized what Vaughan could not—that by then Tyndale's fate was sealed. At any rate, Brussels received no last-minute plea, and in August 1536 Tyndale was sentenced. Had he been released and sent to England, what would have been his fate there? Certainly, he would not have been hailed as a heroic, persecuted Englishman saved from the clasp of the inquisitorial Catholic Church. Many of his views would not have been accepted, and Tyndale was never a man to back down. His death would have been certain, at the least, during the reign of Mary, Henry's daughter. But by then, had he survived, he would have completed the Bible and perhaps a number of revisions.

Maybe it is better that Tyndale was martyred outside of England. It would have been a black spot on that nation to have executed not just the creator of her greatest literary contribution—perhaps her greatest gift of all—but the man who established an English prose that enabled a later genius like Shakespeare to flourish. When Tyndale wrote, English was spoken on an island nation by only a small percentage of the world's population. Now hundreds of millions speak it. It is the mother tongue of two continents and the most well-known second language in the world. It is spoken from India to Hong Kong, from Alaska to New Zealand.

The "Unhallowing"

Because Tyndale was an ordained priest, religious authorities had to publicly degrade him before turning him over to secular powers for his rendezvous with the stake. In a letter dated August 12, 1536, John Hutton, one of Cromwell's agents, reported, "So it is that as the tenth day of this present the procuror-general . . . certified me that William Tyndale is degraded, and condemned into the hands of the secular power, so that he is very like to suffer death this next week."[7]

The degrading took place in Vilvorde and would have included a large number of people, certainly those involved in his examinations, such as Dufief, Masson, and Tapper. Other church authorities most certainly attended as well as leaders from the area. Degradation was also referred to as "unhallowing." It was a public ceremony often held in a church or central square. Tyndale would have been led before the bishops dressed in priestly vestments. After he was forced to kneel, "his hands were scraped with a knife or a piece of glass, as a symbol of the loss of the anointing oil; the bread and the wine were placed in his hands and then taken away" as bishops cursed him with the words, "O cursed Judas, because you have abandoned the counsel of peace . . . we take away from you this cup of redemption." Then "his vestments were stripped from him one by one, and he was clothed in the garments of a layman." A final curse then followed: "We commit your soul to the devil."[8]

Considering Tyndale's attitude toward the clergy and the rites of the priesthood, an attitude he formed while living in England, it is doubtful the ceremony, though humiliating, troubled him. In his letter, Hutton says Tyndale's execution was expected to follow immediately, but it was delayed for two months. Given Tyndale's stature, foreign citizenship, and the fact that the English court had requested his release, authorities no doubt sought approval from the emperor. As the weeks passed relentlessly, the clergy likely attempted to break down Tyndale's resistance and force him to recant so that his soul might be saved.

Like Paul of old, William had "fought a good fight" and "kept the faith." He was "now ready to be offered" and would not waver at the last moment (2 Timothy 4:6–7).

"When His Hour Is Come, Necessity Carrieth Us Hence"

Tyndale was not a relapsed heretic, so he was spared burning alive. His sentence was somewhat merciful in that he was to be strangled before the fires were lit. With the final approvals finally in place, Tyndale was led from his cell on the morning of October 6, 1536. No eyewitness account of his execution has survived, but descriptions of others who suffered the same fate give us an accurate view of his death.

Tyndale was taken to Brussels, where his scaffold was cordoned off by barricades to keep back the crowds of the curious, the sympathetic, and the vengeful. Two large beams were set up in the form of a cross. Chains were fastened to the beams, and a hemp rope was

The martyrdom of William Tyndale.

passed through holes in the beams. Straw, bundles of sticks, and logs were piled around. Prominent seats were prepared for the procurer-general and other commissioners. When the officials were seated and all was ready, Tyndale was led forth through the parting crowds and past the barricades. He was given a moment to pray and recant if he so chose. His prayer over, he walked to the crossed beams, where the guards chained his feet and passed a chain and the hemp rope around his neck. The straw, sticks, and logs were then piled around him, and gunpowder was added to make the flames catch quickly and burn hotter.

The executioner stepped behind Tyndale, looked to the procurer-general, and waited for the signal. At this moment, Foxe reports, Tyndale cried, "Thus at the stake with a fervent zeal, and a loud voice, 'Lord! open the king of England's eyes.'"[9] Even at the last, William Tyndale's thoughts were on the ploughboys and the milk-maids whom he wanted so desperately to know God's word. For them he now sacrificed his life.

The signal was given, and the executioner stepped forward, grabbed the hemp rope, and pulled it tight, silencing the voice and sending the mind that had produced such beauty to its eternal reward. When the procurer-general was sure Tyndale was dead, he handed a lighted torch to the executioner, who set fire to the wood. The great translator was soon enclosed in flame.

A few months later, Cromwell received a letter from his agent, John Hutton. It contained a brief note that read, "They speak much of the patient sufferance of Master Tyndale at the time of his execution."[10] Tyndale had once written to his dear friend John Frith as he approached his own inevitable death, "If you give yourself, cast yourself, yield yourself, commit yourself, wholly and only to your loving Father; then shall his power be in you, and make you strong. . . . There falleth not a hair, till his hour be come; and when his hour is come, necessity carrieth us hence, though we be not willing. But if we be willing, then have we a reward and thank."[11] The pupil had followed the master's council; now the master had been true to his own words.

History has erased the exact location of Tyndale's martyrdom, but Queen Elizabeth's tutor, Roger Ascham, rode through Brussels in 1550 and stopped for a moment of reflection at the place of Tyndale's death. He speaks for all who would stop to ponder the sacrifices of one who enriched our lives so deeply. Writing of his experience a few months later, he said, "At the town's end is a notable solemn place of execution, where worthy William Tyndale was unworthily put to death."[12]

Notes

1. Foxe, *Acts and Monuments*, 5:128.
2. Mozley, *William Tyndale*, 333.
3. Foxe, *Acts and Monuments*, 5:127.
4. Ibid.
5. Mozley, *William Tyndale*, 334–35.
6. Ibid., 320.
7. Ibid., 338.
8. Ibid., 339; see also Moynahan, *God's Bestseller*, 375–76.
9. Foxe, *Acts and Monuments*, 5:127.
10. Mozley, *William Tyndale*, 342.
11. Foxe, *Acts and Monuments*, 5:132.
12. Mozley, *William Tyndale*, 342 n.

"WITH THE KING'S MOST GRACIOUS LICENSE"

Here may all manner of persons: men, women; young, old; learned, unlearned; rich, poor; priests, laymen; lords, ladies; offi-cers, tenants, and mean [average] men; virgins, wives, widows; lawyers, merchants, artificers, husbandmen, and all manner of persons, of what estate or condition soever they be; may in this book learn all things, what they ought to believe, what they ought to do, and what they should not do, as well concerning Almighty God, as also concerning themselves, and all others.

—THOMAS CRANMER, "PREFACE TO THE GREAT BIBLE"

[handwritten margin note: Bible for All]

"BEFORE THEY CALL, I WILL ANSWER"

The Lord promised Isaiah "that before they call, I will answer; and while they are yet speaking, I will hear" (Isaiah 65:24). He was true to his word to his faithful servant William Tyndale, for even as William offered his final prayer at the stake in Brussels, his friend, Miles Coverdale, was busy printing a complete Bible in English. Coverdale was a friend of Thomas Cromwell, who favored a Bible in English and whose influence with Henry was at its height. Anne Boleyn's influence also cannot be min-imized. She owned a deluxe copy of Tyndale's 1534 New Testament, a gift from an Antwerp merchant with the words *Anna Regina Angliae* still faintly seen on its gold edges. The Bible would soon strengthen English nationalism and widen the gap between London and Rome. But Coverdale needed no political motivation or prodding from high officials; his friend was alone in the dark of Vilvorde, and he knew his friend's desires.

In the fall and winter of 1535–36, a full Bible appeared in the streets of London. It was printed on the Continent, shipped to England, and bound by the English printer James Nicolson. Coverdale was not fluent in Greek and Hebrew, but he knew how to take the best from what others had done and was a scholar in his own right. In working with Tyndale, he had learned to tune his ear to the harmony of an English phrase. The New Testament and Pentateuch were Tyndale's, but Coverdale gave us such phrases as "the pride of life," "enter thou into the joy of the Lord," "tender mercies," "respect of persons," "lovingkindness," "the valley of the shadow of death," and the memorable petition from the Lord's Prayer, "and forgive us our debts as we forgive our debtors," which Coverdale altered slightly from Tyndale's rendering.[1]

"LET IT GO ABROAD AMONG OUR PEOPLE"

Coverdale's Bible came to Henry's attention through Thomas Cromwell. Henry immediately asked some of his bishops to read it. Many hesitated to let it circulate freely, citing a number of criticisms, but Henry asked them point-blank, "Well, but are there any heresies maintained thereby?" They admitted there were none. "If there be no heresies, then in God's name let it go abroad among our people."[2] Tyndale and Frith both had promised the king they would remain silent if only he would let a translation of God's word spread among the common people of England. They were both now silent, and the words they gave their lives to hear had finally been spoken by the king.

Coverdale would not put forth his work without giving credit to Tyndale. However, since Tyndale's name was still stained with the mark of heresy, Coverdale could not do so openly. Yet, in his prologue to the reader, he gave a hint, according veiled recognition to Tyndale. Indeed, it was for that man's vision he had undertaken his present labors. Coverdale wrote:

"Considering how excellent knowledge and learning an inter-preter of scripture ought to have in the tongues, and pondering also mine own insufficiency therein, and how weak I am to perform the office of a translator, I was the more loath to meddle with this work. *Notwithstanding when I considered how great pity it was that we should want it so long, and called to my remembrance the adversity of them which were not only of ripe knowledge, but would also with all their hearts have performed that they began, if they had not had impediment: considering (I say) that by reason of their adversity it could not so soon have been brought to an end, as our most prosperous nation would fain have had it: these and other reasonable causes considered, I was the more bold to take it in hand."*[3]

W T

Tyndale's friend John Rogers also knew of his "adversity" and "impediment." Rogers, the chaplain of the English House in Antwerp, was the last person to work with Tyndale. He had some-thing Coverdale lacked—the manuscript copy of Tyndale's transla-tion of the historical books of the Old Testament. Whether he obtained them from Poyntz's wife before the Brussels authorities could confiscate them or knew they were hidden in another spot, he was determined to take advantage of the current atmosphere in England and produce a Bible with all of Tyndale's work included. He too was wary of using Tyndale's name openly or of even using his own for that matter.

Rogers's edition was published in Antwerp under the name Thomas Matthew and has been called Matthew's Bible ever since. Rogers had his own way of bestowing credit where it was due. He placed his initials, "JR," at the end of an exhortation to the reader, and the initials of the English merchants who financed the publica-tion, Richard Grafton and Edward Whitchurch, on the backside of the title page to the prophets. These were done in beautifully fash-ioned letters. He also placed the initials "W T" at the end of Malachi. Large enough to cover half the page, they were also done

Thomas Cranmer.

in elaborate design. It was 1537. Tyndale had been dead but a short time.

Coverdale's version was allowed in England's bookshops by vocal approval of the king, but Archbishop Cranmer and Thomas Cromwell wanted official written sanction for an English Bible and set out to get it. When Matthew's Bible appeared, Cranmer sent it to Cromwell with the following note:

"You shall receive by the bringer hereof a Bible in English, both of a new translation and of a new print. . . . So far as I have read thereof, I like it better than any other translation heretofore made. . . . I pray you, my Lord, that you will exhibit the book unto the king's highness, and to obtain of his Grace, if you can, a license that the same may be sold and read of every person, without danger of any act, proclamation, or ordinance, heretofore granted to the contrary, until such time that we the Bishops shall set forth a better translation, which I think will not be till a day after doomsday."[4]

"The Light Which Every Man Doth See"

Cranmer knew his fellow bishops as well as his king. He was asking Henry to revoke every prohibition to the English Bible back to the Constitutions of Oxford and to allow Tyndale's translation to be acceptable, but only until the bishops produced a "better translation," which he knew would never happen. Effectively, Matthew's Bible would become the official English Bible. That same year, the bishops met in convocation and discussed an English translation. Fierce opposition arose from the more Catholic-leaning bishops, but Cromwell had the upper hand. Bishop John Stokesley, in particular, was adamant that a widely read English Bible would challenge the very pillars of Christendom, but Edward Fox, the bishop of Hereford, calmly arose and turned the tide with cold, clear logic:

"Think ye not that we can, by any sophisticated subtleties, steal out of the world again the light which every man doth see. Christ hath so lightened the world at this time that the light of the Gospel hath put to flight all misty darkness; and it will shortly have the higher hand of all clouds, though we resist in vain never so much. The lay people do now know the Holy Scripture better than many of us. . . . Wherefore, ye must consider earnestly what ye will determine of these controversies, that ye make not yourselves to be mocked and laughed to scorn of all the world."[5]

Hints of Lehi's dream, as well as of Gamaliel's advice to the Pharisees, pervade this passage (1 Nephi 8; Acts 5:34–39). And, of course, we hear Tyndale's own boast given in Little Sodbury a decade earlier that he would see that the ploughboy knew more of the scriptures than the clergy.

IN EVERY PARISH CHURCH

Matthew's Bible, which was at heart Tyndale's Bible, was "set forth with the King's most gracious license." The victory was won! Henry, who had once allowed the fiery destruction of both Tyndale's translations and those who owned them, now officially sanctioned them. Crowds now gathered to the warmth of Tyndale's English instead of the burning of his smuggled pages. Six copies were placed in St. Paul's, the site of so many public burnings. Men would step forward and begin reading to the pressing people. When their voices tired and began to fade, others would take their place as the life of Jesus held the listeners spellbound for hours.

But Cromwell and Archbishop Cranmer were not yet finished. The English Bible should be had in every parish church across the realm, including the smallest rural chapel, where those who could not purchase their own could still hear the flowing cadences and cryptic truths so admirably expressed by one of England's greatest native sons.

Some of the marginal notes in Matthew's Bible, however, were not popular with many of the realm's clergy. So Coverdale was approached and asked to produce a new Bible, drawing upon the best from both his own edition and the Matthew's Bible edition. Coverdale did his work in France with one of Europe's most skilled printers, but the French inquisition caught wind of it, forcing him to use bribes and smuggling techniques polished during darker days. After the printed sheets had been safely delivered as "waste paper" in England, Cromwell bought the press and type and hired the original printers to finish the job in England.

In 1539, the Great Bible was completed, so called because of its size—small enough to fit comfortably on the pulpit of a parish church but large enough for all to see its conspicuous presence. Its title page carried a hidden tribute to its major contributor: "The Bible in English . . . truly translated after the verity of the Hebrew and Greek texts, by the diligent study of diverse excellent learned men, expert in the foresaid tongues."[6]

This version was also sponsored by Grafton and Whitchurch. Through Cromwell's influence, Henry ordered the clergy to see that "one book of the whole Bible, of the largest volume, in English, and the same set up in some convenient place within the said church that you have cure of [responsibility for], whereat your parishioners may most commodiously resort to the same and read it."[7]

In 1526, Tyndale's New Testament was burned at St. Paul's; now his words were placed in every parish church. Furthermore, the clergy were to "expressly provoke, stir and exhort every person to read the same, as that which is the very lively Word of God."[8]

The Rod for the "Yoke" of Iron

How did the people in the villages and towns respond to their new English Bible? As in London, they crowded the churches to read and discuss the truths they found therein. Throngs became so thick and the services and sermons so often ignored that Henry issued another edict requesting his people to benefit from the new Great Bible "most humbly and reverently," using it "quietly and charitably every [one] of you to the edifying of himself, his wife and family."[9] So great was the desire to know truth fresh from its source that the new Bible encouraged literacy among the people. The rod of iron was replacing the "yoke of iron" that had held men in "captivity" for so many dark centuries (1 Nephi 13:5). In 1611, the King James Version took as its foundation and core Tyndale's work.

Tyndale published his first New Testament without adding his name because he wanted to follow his Savior's command to do good works without the left hand knowing what the right hand was doing. He would not have been troubled by the fact that the crowds of common folk who massed around his translations did not know to whom they owed such a debt of gratitude. Nephi was once told, "It is better that one man should perish than that a nation should dwindle and perish in unbelief" (1 Nephi 4:13). In a reverse application of the Spirit's words, one man had perished—doing so because his nation had lingered long enough in the dark world of unbelief and because the light of God's words could not forever be locked in the prison of dead languages, clerical ignorance, and blind authority.

We must not let his name perish from the conscious memory of those who love the Bible's reverberating words, so melodiously rendered in the simple, plain speech of the common man—words that have lifted and inspired the English race for five centuries.

NOTES

1. Bobrick, *Wide As the Waters*, 145.
2. Bruce, *History of the Bible*, 55–56.
3. Ibid., 57–58.
4. Price, *Ancestry of Our English Bible*, 255.
5. Bobrick, *Wide As the Waters*, 147.
6. Price, *Ancestry of Our English Bible*, 256–57; spelling standardized.
7. Ibid., 258; spelling standardized.
8. Bruce, *History of the Bible*, 68.
9. Price, *Ancestry of Our English Bible*, 259.

AS THE
YEARS PASSED

After most humble recommendation I do pray your grace to understand that I am accumbred [burdened] with such as keepeth and readeth these erroneous books in English, and believe and give credence to the same, and teacheth others that they should do so. My Lord I have done that lieth in me for the suppression of such persons, but it passeth my power, or any spiritual man to do it.

—Bishop Nix of Norwich, Letter to
Archbishop Warham, May 14, 1530

ROBERT BARNES

Robert Barnes carried a bundle of sticks to St. Paul's Cross in 1526 and lived in exile for years afterward. He was one of the men Henry Phillips plotted to arrest. He was condemned as a heretic during the fall of Thomas Cromwell and burned with two companions at Smithfield on July 30, 1540. Even with the Bible in free circulation, England in the mid-sixteenth century was not safe for reformers.

ANNE BOLEYN

After the death of Catherine of Aragon, Anne Boleyn quickly fell from Henry's favor. When she had a stillborn son shortly thereafter, her fate was sealed. After Henry became infatuated with Jane Seymour, Anne was accused of adultery. On May 19, 1536, she was beheaded in the French manner (sword instead of ax). With her death, the reforming spirit took a blow. Archbishop Cranmer wrote to Henry of her, "I loved her not a little, for the love which I judged her to bear towards God and his gospel."[1] Her copy of Tyndale's 1534 New Testament is located in the British Library.

MILES COVERDALE

Miles Coverdale, assistant to Tyndale in Hamburg while he worked on the Pentateuch and who published the Bible after Tyndale's imprisonment, became a wandering preacher for a number of years. Unable to conform to certain features of the Anglican Settlement—a compromise between Protestantism and Catholicism reached under Elizabeth—he died in poverty on May 26, 1569.

THOMAS CRANMER

Archbishop Thomas Cranmer recanted during the persecutions against the Protestants during the reign of Queen Mary. Like so many of the early reformers, his conscience troubled him so deeply that he staged a dramatic meeting in Oxford to disavow his former weakness. His prayer before his death, wherein he said, "Thou didst not give Thy Son, O Heavenly Father, unto death for small sins only, but for all the greatest sins of the world, so that the sinner return to Thee with his whole heart, as I do at present" is one of the most moving moments in reform history.[2] He was burned at Oxford on March 21, 1556, placing the hand he had used to sign his recantation into the flames first.

THOMAS CROMWELL

Thomas Cromwell's climb to the heights of power did not last long. He angered Henry for arranging an unsatisfactory marriage to Anne of Cleves, from Germany, and for pushing reform too rapidly. Accused of treason, he was beheaded on July 28, 1540. Before his death, he remarked to Lord Hungerford, who was executed the same day, "Though the breakfast which we are going to, be sharp, yet, trusting to the mercy of the Lord, we shall have a joyful dinner."[3] Though portrayed as the villain in *A Man for All Seasons,* he was one of the reformers' true friends.

ERASMUS

Erasmus of Rotterdam, whose writings profoundly motivated young William Tyndale and fueled his inspiration to make the scriptures available to all, died quietly the night of July 11, 1536. Despite his desires to see the Catholic Church reformed, he remained true to Catholicism throughout his life. Beloved for his learning and gentle manner, Erasmus was not the material of which martyrs are made. Mozley sums up his life best by comparing his humanist ways with the moral fiber of Tyndale:

"The victory went to those who were the more worthy of it. With all their mistakes, the reformers showed a grit and a driving force, a moral backbone, which was lacking in the humanists. They launched their boat in swirling waters; they risked their lives to purge the church; they lived dangerously and whole-heartedly, and they had their reward. . . . If apt and well-aimed words could have reformed the church, Erasmus would have reformed it. None saw the need more clearly than he. . . . But his deeds were not correspondent with his words. He sat still, and let things take their course. . . . Sterner souls . . . rode the storm on which he feared to venture."[4]

JOHN FISHER

Bishop John Fisher fully supported the offensive against Tyndale and the reformers, preaching railing sermons at St. Paul's before cowering men condemned to carry bundles of sticks. He strongly opposed Henry's divorce and found himself on the short list of Cromwell's enemies. A friend and supporter of Sir Thomas More, he was one of the few bishops who refused to sign the Oath of Succession, which acknowledged the legitimacy of Henry's marriage to Anne Boleyn. Accused of treason, he was placed in the Tower of London at the same time as Sir Thomas and was later beheaded on Tower Hill. At the time, he was so weak from his imprisonment that he had to be carried to his execution.

JOHN FOXE

John Foxe went into exile with many other English Protestants during Queen Mary's persecution. Upon the accession of Elizabeth, he returned to England. His comprehensive work on the martyrs took eleven years. He did all of the research himself, refusing to use a scribe and sacrificing his health to the point that many of his acquaintances no longer recognized him. He died on April 18, 1587, sending away his two sons beforehand to spare them the grief of his passing.

HENRY VIII

Henry's religious whims wavered as much as his choice in wives. With the fall of Cromwell, the antireforming party got the upper hand, and Parliament condemned "the crafty, false and untrue translation of Tyndale," forbidding the lay people from reading the Bible. Bibles were again burned in public places, but with true irony the Great Bible, which contained all of Tyndale, still sat comfortably on parish pulpits as the appointed version of the nation. During the waning days of Henry's reign, Robert Williams, from Tyndale's own Gloucestershire, wrote in 1546: "When I kept Mr. Latimer's sheep I bought this book when the testament was obberagated [banned] that sheep herds might not read it. I pray God amend that blindness."[5] Tyndale surely would have smiled to see a Gloucestershire shepherd sitting on a hill reading his translation of the Good Shepherd. Henry died January 28, 1547. With all his faults and misguided, selfish motives, he was the first English king to allow the Bible to be printed in English. His daughter Elizabeth, besides becoming the most celebrated monarch in English history, permanently established the English Reformation.

GEORGE JOYE

George Joye was suspected of aiding Henry Phillips, but the charges were unfounded, and he remained true to the reforming spirit to the end of his life. He continued to publish various scriptural translations of the Old Testament, returning to England and then fleeing again depending on the religious climate. He married, had eight children, and died in England in 1553, just before Queen Mary's persecutions, which certainly would have sent him into exile again if not to the stake. He produced such scriptural gems as "pride goeth before a fall" and "a mess of pottage."

THOMAS MORE

Henry VIII beheaded Sir Thomas More on July 7, 1535, for refusing to take an oath supporting the king's position as head of the church in England. In 1935, he was declared a saint by the Roman Catholic Church, the first English layman to be so honored. In 2000, he became the patron saint for politicians. His life was the subject of Robert Bolt's riveting play that was made into the movie *A Man for All Seasons,* which won six academy awards in 1966, including Best Picture.

HENRY PHILLIPS

After betraying Tyndale, Henry Phillips wandered from city to city on the Continent, including Rome, but could find no patron or city that would welcome him. He lived a life of perpetual poverty, always begging for money. True to his character, he stole from those who took him into their confidence or tried to help him. Foxe indicated, "This Phillips rejoiced awhile after he had done it [betrayed Tyndale], yet the saying so goeth, that he not long time after enjoyed

The burning of John Rogers.

the price of innocent blood, but was consumed at last with lice."[6] The only significance attached to his name is his one scheming, perfidious deed.

Thomas Poyntz

Thomas Poyntz, Tyndale's untiring friend, lost all in his attempt to save Tyndale. Banished from the Low Countries after his escape, he remained in England. His wife, Anna van Calva, a native of Antwerp, refused to leave her city and join him, thus parting him from his children. After his brother's death in 1547, he inherited the family estate in North Ockenden, Essex, but his debts were so heavy from his imprisonment that poverty remained his fate. He was buried at a parish church with the following epitaph, translated from Latin: "He, for faithful service to his prince and ardent profession of evangelical truth, suffered bonds and imprisonment beyond the sea, and would plainly have been destined to death, had he not, trusting in divine providence, saved himself in a wonderful manner by breaking his prison. In this chapel he now sleeps peacefully in the Lord, 1562."[7]

John Rogers

John Rogers, alias Thomas Matthew, saw Tyndale's translations into print. He returned to England and was condemned as a heretic during the reign of Queen Mary, who zealously tried to return England to the Catholic fold. He was the first to die under her hand, meeting death at the stake in February 1555. Rogers was forbidden to see his wife before he died. She and their eleven children, one a baby in arms, stood along the road as he went to his death.

William Roye

William Roye, Tyndale's somewhat unwelcome helper in Cologne and Worms who published embarrassing rhymes that offended Tyndale, later traveled to Portugal, where both More and

Foxe report that he was burned at the stake in 1531. Though not highly spoken of by Tyndale, Roye showed courage and carried the conviction of his beliefs to the end.

John Stokesley

Bishop John Stokesley, nicknamed "the hammer of heretics," remained an ardent defender of the old faith until his death, although he did go along with Henry VIII's Act of Supremacy. He had the persecuting zeal of Sir Thomas More but lacked the martyr's courage. When asked by Archbishop Cranmer to help prepare a sanctioned edition of the Bible in English, he refused to have anything to do with the project. After he was assigned the Book of Acts, he wrote Cranmer, "I marvel what my Lord of Canterbury meaneth that thus abuseth the people in giving them liberty to read the scripture. . . . I have bestowed never an hour on my portion, nor never will."[8] Stokesley, who christened Anne Boleyn's daughter, Elizabeth, died on September 8, 1539.

Cuthbert Tunstall

Bishop Cuthbert Tunstall, who rejected Tyndale's request for permission to translate the New Testament before he went into exile, burned his books, and assigned Thomas More to refute them, became bishop of Durham. In 1541, he affixed his name to the Great Bible, thus sanctioning all for which Tyndale had lived and died, with the words: "Overseen and perused at the commandment of the King's Highness by the right reverend fathers in God." At Tunstall's death, Erasmus wrote of him, "Our age does not possess a man more learned, a better or a kinder man."[9] To his credit, Tunstall refused to burn heretics.

Stephen Vaughan

Because of his praise and defense of Tyndale, Vaughan came under suspicion and greatly feared for his life. Several of his surviving letters show his fear of Sir Thomas More. He was no reformer, but he spoke up for Tyndale at the risk of his own standing. In a letter to Cromwell, he wrote in a tolerant tone not shared by many of his contemporaries. "Yea, and whereas they think that tortures, punishments and death shall be a mean to rid the realm of erroneous opinions, and bring men in such fear that they shall not once be so hardy to speak or look; be you assured, and let the king's grace be thereof advertised of my mouth, that his highness shall duly approve [make proof] that in the end it shall cause the sect to wax greater, and those errors to be more plenteously sowed in the realm than ever afore."[10] Vaughan became a member of Parliament before his death in 1549.

THE PLOUGHBOY

Tyndale's ploughboy has made the English Bible the most widely read book in the history of the world and its largely unknown translator the most quoted since the Creation.

NOTES

1. Moynahan, *God's Bestseller,* 370.
2. Foxe, *Book of Martyrs,* 248.
3. Foxe, *Acts and Monuments,* 5:438.
4. Mozley, *William Tyndale,* 236–37.
5. Bruce, *History of the Bible,* 79.
6. Foxe, *Acts and Monuments,* 5:129.
7. Mozley, *William Tyndale,* 319.
8. Moynahan, *God's Bestseller,* 385; spelling standardized.
9. Ibid., 37.
10. Campbell, *Erasmus, Tyndale, and More,* 200.

BIBLIOGRAPHY

Ackroyd, Peter. *The Life of Thomas More.* New York: Nan A. Talese, 1998.

Andrus, Hyrum and Helen Mae. *They Knew the Prophet.* Salt Lake City: Bookcraft, 1974.

Bainton, Roland, H. *Here I Stand—A Life of Martin Luther.* Nashville, Tenn.: Abingdon Press, 1950.

Bobrick, Benson. *Wide As the Waters: The Story of the English Bible and the Revolution It Inspired.* New York: Simon & Schuster, 2001.

Bolt, Robert. *A Man for All Seasons.* New York: Scholastic Book Services, 1960.

Bruce, F. F. *History of the Bible in English.* 3d ed. Oxford, England: Oxford University Press, 1978.

The Cambridge History of the Bible. 3 vols. Volume 3 edited by S. L. Greenslade. Cambridge, England: University Press, 1963.

Campbell, W. E. *Erasmus, Tyndale, and More.* Milwaukee, Wisc.: Bruce Publishing, [1950].

Cavendish, George, and William Roper. *Two Early Tudor Lives: The Life and Death of Cardinal Wolsey/The Life of Sir Thomas More.* New Haven, Conn.: Yale University Press, 1962.

Daniell, David. *William Tyndale: A Biography.* New Haven, Conn.: Yale University Press, 1994.

————. *Tyndale's New Testament.* New Haven, Conn.: Yale University Press, 1989.

————. *Tyndale's Old Testament.* New Haven, Conn.: Yale University Press, 1992.

Dickens, A. G. *The English Reformation.* 2d ed. London: Batsford, 1989.

Duffield, G. E. *The Work of William Tyndale.* Philadelphia: Fortress Press, 1965.

Eight Translation New Testament. Wheaton, Ill.: Tyndale House Publishers, Inc., 1987.

BIBLIOGRAPHY

Erasmus. *Enchiridion Militis Christiani: An English Version.* Edited by Anne M. O'Donnell. Oxford, England: Oxford University Press, 1981.

Foxe, John. *The Acts and Monuments of John Foxe: With a Life of the Martyrologist, and Vindication of the Work.* Edited by George Townsend. 8 vols. New York: AMS Press Inc., 1965.

———. *Fox's Book of Martyrs: A History of the Lives, Sufferings and Triumphant Deaths of the Early Christian and the Protestant Martyrs.* Edited by William Byron Forbush. Philadelphia: John C. Winston Company, 1926.

Greenslade, S. L. *The Work of William Tindale.* London: Blackie & Son Limited, 1938.

Hall, Edward. *Hall's Chronicle: Containing a History of England.* 1809.

Hymns of The Church of Jesus Christ of Latter-day Saints. Salt Lake City: The Church of Jesus Christ of Latter-day Saints, 1985.

King, Arthur Henry. *The Abundance of the Heart.* Salt Lake City: Bookcraft, 1986.

Levi, Peter. *The English Bible.* Grand Rapids, Mich.: William B. Eerdmans Publishing, 1974.

More, Thomas. *The Complete Works of St. Thomas More.* 15 vols. New Haven, Conn.: Yale University Press, 1963.

Moynahan, Brian. *God's Bestseller: William Tyndale, Thomas More, and the Writing of the English Bible.* New York: St. Martin's Press, 2003.

Mozley, J. F. *William Tyndale.* New York: MacMillan, 1937.

The Oxford English Dictionary. Edited by James A. H. Murray, et al. 12 vols. Oxford, England: Clarendon Press, 1933.

Price, Ira Maurice. *The Ancestry of Our English Bible.* 2d ed. rev. New York: Harper & Brothers, 1949.

Quinn, Arthur. *Figures of Speech.* Salt Lake City: Peregrine Smith Books, 1982.

Rheims. *The New Testament of Jesus Christ translated faithfully into English, out of the authentical Latin.* 1582.

Roper, William. *The Life of Sir Thomas More.* Book 2 in *Two Early Tudor Lives.* Edited by Richard S. Sylvester and Davis P. Harding. New Haven, Conn.: Yale University Press, 1962.

Smith, Joseph. *History of The Church of Jesus Christ of Latter-day Saints.* Edited by B. H. Roberts. 2d ed. rev. 7 vols. Salt Lake City: The Church of Jesus Christ of Latter-day Saints, 1932–51.

BIBLIOGRAPHY

Tyndale, William. *New Testament 1526.* Edited by F. F. Bruce. 450th anniversary edition. From the Library of Baptist College, Bristol, England, 1976.

————. *The Practice of Prelates.* Edited by Henry Walker. The Parker Society Edition, 1849.

Webster's Word Histories. Edited by Frederick C. Mish. Springfield, Mass.: Merriam-Webster Inc., 1989.

Williamson, David. *Kings and Queens of England.* New York: Barnes & Noble, 1998.

Word, Church, and State—Tyndale Quincentenary Essays. Edited by John T. Day, Eric Lund, and Anne M. O'Donnell. Washington, D.C.: Catholic University of America Press, 1998.

The World Book Dictionary. Edited by Clarence L. Barnhart. Chicago: Field Enterprises Educational Corp., 1963.

INDEX

E

F

ℳ